D1321807

STONES OF FIRE

ISOBEL KUHN

STONES
OF FIRE

"... upon the holy mountain
of God, thou hast walked up
and down in the midst of the
stones of fire" (Ezekiel 28.14)

Foreword by John B. Kuhn

OMF BOOKS

©OVERSEAS MISSIONARY FELLOWSHIP
(formerly China Inland Mission)

First published *1951*
Fourteen reprints *1961-1980*
Reprinted *1984*

ISBN 9971−972−00−X

OMF Books are distributed by
OMF, 404 South Church Street,
Robesonia, Pa. 19551, USA.
and OMF, Belmont, The Vine,
Sevenoaks, Kent, TN13 3TZ, UK
and other OMF offices.

Cover photo by Macquitty International Collection

Published by Overseas Missionary Fellowship (IHQ) Ltd.,
2 Cluny Road, Singapore 1025, Republic of Singapore
Printed by Hiap Seng Press Pte. Ltd., Singapore

Contents

	Page
Foreword	7
Prelude	13
1. A Stone is Quarried	17
2. Stones in His Pocket	25
3. A Stone Selected	41
4. Two Stones are Set Together	54
5. War—as Diamond Dust	64
6. The Climax of the Lapidary's Skill	92
7. Made only of Desert Dust	106
8. The Communist Stone of Fire	136
9. From His Pocket to His Crown	150

Foreword

by John B. Kuhn

A DECADE has passed since that memorable farewell day along the Salween River! Isobel and six-year-old Daniel departed for the United States while I remained to continue on a while longer; how long, only the Lord knew. We had hoped to reunite in China again after Dan was happily settled at school in the homeland. Events soon revealed, however, that such was not to be the case. At the close of 1950 the Mission directive was received which effected withdrawal from China. I broke the news very gently to a small company of Lisu Christians as we rested on the hillside en route to our official's residence. "We are making plans to leave the country," said I quietly, to the men seated around Charles Peterson and me. Just as quietly one replied from their midst: "I think you'll be back after five years." No one knew but we all hoped so. Ten years have now elapsed and our prospect of such reunion is as remote as it was then.

My loved ones reached the United States and together with daughter Kathryn they settled in Wheaton, in the state of Illinois. But life in Lisuland continued apace and there was plenty to occupy one. As the growing sense of the shortness of time impressed us, the urgency of the present task bore down upon us. There was necessary itineration among the churches for Bible teaching, the pressure of translation work and the ever present claims in the wider oversight of the Mission's work in west Yunnan. They were days of great opportunity and of widespread ministry and even though a year and nine months passed before we were joyously reunited as a complete family in Wheaton, there was little time left to think upon our long separation. In those months of waiting for permission to leave China there were periods in which we were expected to think upon ourselves, but then too we found Christ our constant portion and our all-sufficiency.

With China closed, the Lord opened the door to Thailand where we served in the northern arc in the interests of the many tribes to be found there. Here the Lord marvellously supplied missionaries for each remaining tribe and people needing to hear the Gospel. The Blue Meo, White Meo, the Lahu, Shan, Pwo Karen, Lisu, Yao and Aka were each in turn provided with their own missionaries and our slogan ran:

> To every Tribe the Living Word
> In every Tribe a Living Church.

Then Isobel received the doctor's verdict: Cancer. After surgery in McCormick Hospital at Chiengmai she was flown to New York and reunited with Kathy and Dan in Philadelphia. I remained on the field to finish out the term of service. This gave us another separation from November 1954 to September 1955. During these months, daughter Kathy came forward to the field as a missionary, leaving home with the full consent of her mother, even though it was by then apparent that they would never again meet on earth. I was on the dock to meet Kathy in Singapore that beautiful Easter Sunday which was her twenty-fourth birthday. We had the cheer of being in the same city for the following few months, Kathy in language study preparatory to work in Thailand and I serving temporarily at headquarters. At the end of August 1955, Kathy waved me off aboard a Pan-American plane headed for Manila and thence to U.S.A. Within a few days Isobel and I had the great joy of reunion.

We lived in Wheaton from then on until the Lord called her home on 20 March, 1957. It was during this period that Isobel did her most fruitful writing: *Ascent to the Tribes*, *By Searching*, *Green Leaf in Drought* and *In the Arena* and also the personal writings bound up in *One Vision Only* all took shape during those months of waning strength. We who stood and served marvelled at the grace of God displayed daily as life slowly withdrew from this earthly scene into the presence of Him whom she declared was her "Alpha and Omega". Isobel slipped away from us in a series of surrenders. First, and long after she was entirely confined to bed, she surrendered the *pen.* As was her rule of life, she did this uncomplainingly. Letters, books, notes, all done. People have wondered about Isobel's gift for writing. What was the secret? Was it basic training? Was it spiritual gift? Was it natural talent? It may have been something from all of these, but my personal opinion gained from close observation over a quarter of a century is that it was developed from the practice of writing. In 1934 she began to portray the Lisu work in regular monthly letters to a limited circle of interested friends at home. The inspiration for this came through the example of Mr. J. O. Fraser who carried on a similar plan of writing in his pioneer ministry among the Lisu tribe of south-west China. Thus Isobel's monthly "Prayer Trust" was regularly written throughout the years. Sometimes these letters were lengthy but usually they carried fresh forthright impressions of thrilling close-up life as she experienced or observed it. From this practice of letter writing came very naturally and simply the art of writing books, so that much of Isobel's permanent works to-day are made up of former writings in letters down through the years.

There was another inspiration for book-writing which early came to her through the Mission. It came by way of a circular written by Frank Houghton, intended to stir missionaries up to writing. Bishop Houghton was then editorial secretary in the London office of the C.I.M. His enthusiasm and encouragement gripped Isobel's imagination and she took up her pen. The result was a compilation of chapters under the title of *Comrades of the Second Mile* which she sent to Bishop Houghton who was then travelling in inland China. The book was turned down! It included allusions to too many missionaries then living, which was thought rather unwise. Hence, the book never appeared in print, but Bishop Houghton gave timely and wise counsel and encouraged her to continue to write. She did. In due course, *Precious Things of the Lasting Hills* appeared. Other succeeding editorial secretaries have continued the Bishop's strategy of encouragement and to them is due much credit for their constant support in the publication of the various books which subsequently appeared.

Secondly, there was the surrender of the *Lisu prayer time.*

This was observed regularly through the years in the early afternoon at which time the Lisu church was prayed for. Here the prayer battle for precious Lisu Christian lives was fought. Notes were kept of names and needs spread over the field, and these were regularly brought before the Lord in prayer. Isobel made her "Prayer Trust" letters challenge her own heart first, and continually, and only then could she rightly expect others to be challenged. Thus prayer for the field each afternoon was a time sacred, and needed to be guarded and diligently kept. However, strength gave way and the time for such exacting work was ending. Quietly, serenely, she surrendered the Lisu prayer time.

Thirdly, she surrendered *Dan*. Only mother and son were together on that last afternoon as they took leave of each other. Even as two years before she had graciously, if not calmly, bid farewell to daughter Kathryn for service as a "sent one" to the "regions beyond", she was now taking leave of our son. She and Dan were very close to each other. His sweet presence was real down through the years. He was there now, but eternity alone will unveil the sacred breathings of that hour.

Then lastly, *life itself*. Only Dad and Mother were together on that last morning. We had read and prayed. Then suddenly the end was near. Quietly, patiently, with the sense of His presence so near, she crossed "the last defile". Mummy left us at fifty-four years of age, yet as we laid her to rest it was with the assurance that it was not a premature death but rather that of a triumphantly fulfilled life!

God has been pleased to bless her writings beyond our most fanciful dreams. *By Searching* has reached the 100,000 mark alone. Constantly we receive testimonies to the blessing this book has been to individual lives. This fact, together with the story itself, is justification for the reprinting of *Stones of Fire*. The first edition has long since been exhausted and we pray that this new edition will meet with acceptance ordained unto blessing.

Meanwhile, the Lisu Church has moved forward. Ten years have seen many Christians cross the mountains at the frontier and re-establish themselves in Burma. In September 1958 I visited some of them. 143-strong came to welcome us at the missionary's residence in Myitkyina in Upper Burma. There were Luke, Jeremiah, Barnabas and many others of personal acquaintance of China days! Overwhelming! "Let us sing," and Pastor Luke as of yore led in the same old characteristically bright hymn singing as only the Lisu Christians can do. Our hearts were touched.

"How long are you going to be with us, Ma-pa?"

"Ten-odd days."

"Fine, we are having our Bible Conference in the nearby village just now and we wish you to speak to us."

"Very well. I'm your servant for the time we're here."

Soon we were transported to the Lisu part of Mankhring Kachin village and comfortably set up in a Lisu Christian home. Soon they had me in harness: four periods of preaching and teaching each day, before breakfast, after breakfast, afternoon and evening. The Lisu language was soon in smooth running order and we were once again enjoying the ministry of the Word in the Lisu tongue to hearts that were hungry for it. Many of the friends gathered at the airport to sing us farewell.

The work of the Lisu Church goes on. Each separate district in north Burma has its own teacher to care for the village churches. The annual Bible conference keeps them in close touch with one another. The periodical *Spiritual Food* magazine helps them to grow. This is produced by a number of their former China missionaries who later served in Thailand. Then there is the eager expectation of soon possessing the whole Bible in the Lisu tongue. How well I remember on one occasion Lucius Ju (Lu-seng) declaring before the church in a public address that he would never be satisfied until he had the whole Bible in his own tongue. This is now happily in view as the translators have collaborated in translation during these recent years in north Thailand. The aim has been to have the whole Lisu Bible in the hands of the church of this generation. For the completion of this great task we and the Lisu Church shall ever be grateful to God for the painstaking services of Allyn Cooke and Allan Crane, and as well to teachers Job Fish and Chao-Ta, and others who have collaborated in this work.

Our prayer as this new impression of *Stones of Fire* goes forward is that the Lisu Church, whether in China or Burma, may continue steadfastly in the truth which the pioneers and missionaries have taught her and ever reach out towards those who still grope in darkness and the shadow of death.

Prelude

STONES of fire. The first time I ever saw them was in a
setting as unique as unexpected.

It happened many years ago, in the days of youthful agnosti-
cism, and while I was travelling with the Players Club of our
university. A yachting club had sponsored our play that night,
and after the performance they gave us a dance at their clubhouse
on the waters of a lovely lake.

A member of the club, appointed as partner and until then
unknown to me, said, as the orchestra ceased playing, "Come
out to the verandah a moment. I want to show you something."
Dancing up to the clubhouse door which opened on to a bal-
cony over the lake, he led me out to the unlit piazza. Electric
light from the ballroom streamed through the doorway, whilst
out on the lake the moon was making a softer brilliance on the
rippling waters. Giving a quick glance at my puzzled face, this
strange man thrust his hand into his pocket, pulled out something, and held it in the light from the doorway for me to
look at.

"Have you ever seen anything like this?" he inquired. On
his open palm lay about ten little pale stones, but as I gazed I
became entranced, for each little stone was shooting fire—ruby
lights, emerald lights, golden lights, amethyst—they were
indescribable. It was as if tiny living rainbows had been captured
and put into pale translucent prisons from which they were
sending forth rays of fire. I was enthralled.

"Oh, how beautiful! What are they?" I cried.

"Mexican opals," my partner replied casually. "I like them,
and so I carry them loose in my pocket. I like to put my hand
down and feel them, even if there is not time to take them out
and look at them. I carry them with me wherever I go."

That was all; but I never forgot those beautiful stones.

Not long after that, Christ challenged me and I yielded. In
course of time He took me to the end of the earth, and there, in

a setting as unique and as unexpected as in the first instance, I found the living counterpart of the little opals from that scene of my youth.

The pocket this time was a canyon, thousands of feet deep in mother earth, tucked into the foothills of the Tibetan plateau. The gems were simple unpretentious tribesfolk, rock-like in their fidelities but flashing fire if the depths of their love were touched.

Stones of fire. While watching them battle with untoward circumstance, the analogy dawned on me, sweeping me back a quarter of a century in time and over half the world in space. But there it was, perfect.

"Upon the holy mountain of God thou hast walked up and down in the midst of the stones of fire." Ezek. 28:14.

Let us look at them in the light of a comment from Dr. Campbell Morgan: "What a strange bringing together of contradictions! 'Stones of fire'. A stone is the last embodiment of principle—hard and cold. Fire is the essence of passion—warm and energizing. Put the two together, and we have stones—principle; fire—passion; principle shot through with passion, passion held by principle." That is the description of a human stone of fire.

At the end of the earth, where mountains are flung peak upon peak, as if they were discards of the Creator, piled together chaotically, the Salween River carves its way through the granite masses making a canyon thousands of feet deep. As the side-veinings of a leaf meet at the centre vein, so hundreds of tributaries into the Salween have cut abysmal ravines in the western and eastern banks of the Green River, as the Chinese call it. And so this canyon with its tributary ravines have netted the mountain range into hundreds of slopes on which the wild needle-grass grows profusely. For unknown centuries the Lisu tribespeople have ploughed these perpendicular hillsides into cornfields and reaped a bare, rough living.

The Chinese contemptuously refer to them as "earth people" and have noticed them only to collect taxes, for which purpose a magistrate lives at Luchang town. For the rest, the canyon is governed by the feudal system; the landowners (designated in this book by the Scottish term *lairds*), are the real rulers of the people, and how they rule will be revealed as the story unfolds.

To the east there is the parallel canyon of the great Mekong River, through which the Lisu salt-traders must go to get to the salt mines. For the rest, civilization as we know it—shops, telegraph, medical clinics, and so on—is many days' journey away. Paoshan City, supply base of the missionary, is about a week's travel from the scene of this narrative.

The story of how the Lisu tribe was first evangelized is told in *Behind the Ranges*;[1] and of how the Upper Salween was opened to the gospel, in *Nests Above the Abyss*.[2]

Now I would step aside and let you see God, the great Lapidary, as He takes up a clod of earth and forms it into a jewel; selects a little earth-person and makes her into a *stone of fire*.

[1] *Behind the Ranges: Fraser of Lisuland*, by Mrs. Howard Taylor.
[2] *Nests above the Abyss*, by Isobel Kuhn (*out of print*).

1

A Stone is Quarried

A SMALL figure was toiling up the orange mud of the long mountain road. In that canyon where human beings, so undernourished, mature slowly, she looked about ten or twelve years of age, whereas in reality she was fifteen. The day was warm and the big load of firewood in the basket on her back was heavy, so she paused to rest it on a rock that jutted out of the road bank. Pulling out the end of her dark blue turban, she wiped the perspiration from her face, then as she tucked it back in place, her eye caught a glimpse of another figure coming up the road behind her. Tall, young, unburdened, he was swinging over the ground with a graceful lilt which would soon overtake her.

"Born-on-the-Road." The little girl murmured his name to herself. "He must be home for the week-end from Bible School." Then as she watched the gloss of his carefully groomed curly black hair, she thought within herself, "I'll take another look when he has passed." A general favourite was Born-on-the-Road. But as the young Bible student swung up to the little wood-carrier he stopped to talk.

"Third Sister, have you never thought of believing in Jesus?"

Confused and embarrassed at direct conversation from this young Adonis, the little girl blushed, dropped her eyes and said shyly, "Father would not let me."

"But this is not a matter in which you should listen to your father! As we Lisu say, 'The one who eats is the one who gets full.' You have a soul and God's Son, Jesus, died to save your soul from hell. If you believe, and accept Him as your Saviour, God gives you eternal life, and your father cannot take it away from you or keep it from you. But God forces His gift on no one.

You must decide; you, and you only. If you decide to accept, God will take care of your father. You think that over and make your own decision."

Seeing that she was too scared and timid to even look at him, he strode off ahead, his bookbag slung over his shoulder swaying colourfully with the swing of his lithe form. But this was the first touch of the pickaxe on this little stone which was to remove it from the mountain of heathenism into its new home. How little either of them thought that day of what the future would bring into their two lives.

All the way up the long winding trail to Village of the Olives, Third Sister was debating, as she carried her heavy load. She would like to please her exhorter, for if there was one person in the world that she admired it was Born-on-the-Road. All the village knew that he was clean and true; knew too the testings which had taken place since his conversion six years before. At the time of that event, she herself had been but eight years of age; however, she could still remember the stir among the adults of the village when that first Lisu evangelist, Isaiah, had come to Olives, and said it was wrong to worship demons. Born-on-the-Road's family were the first to cast out their demon altar.

Born-on-the-Road was not his real name; it was the village's nickname in memory of his entrance into the world. As Third Sister came trotting around the curve, she could see the high rock where his birth had taken place. Although his mother had endeavoured to reach home from her work in the rice-fields that evening, the baby had come on the trail beneath that great cliff. His parents had named him Ju-fah-gwey, but the village folk refused to call him by it. Lu-seng (the Chinese for Born-on-the-Road) he was, and Lu-seng-pa was his father and Lu-seng-ma was his mother, and must be until they died!

"Yes; how good it would be to become a Christian," mused Third Sister as she pattered along at the wood-carriers jog-trot. She now had a full view of their village with the small white chapel built in the middle of Lu-seng's farm. "But Father would never let me go there. Oh no. Why, Second Sister is a secret Christian, and look what a time she has of it! But then, if I became one too, we could stand together, perhaps. . . ." But even so, what were women in this land where every female is but chattel in some man's hand all her days? Thus debating the matter, the little fifteen-year-old arrived at her home.

*   *   *

Many months passed. Third Sister was busy for already she was learning to spin cotton into thread and then weave it into cloth on the primitive foot-loom. This was the women's winter work, besides the inevitable gathering firewood, pounding corn and the daily water carrying.

Lu-seng had gone with Ma-pa and Ma-ma (the white missionaries) up to Village of the Three Clans where the Lord had begun a mighty work. Olives is on the main road south to Chinaland, so Lisu traders coming from the north often brought letters from Lu-seng to the church at Olives. Second Sister went secretly to church and on returning home would wait until they were alone and then recount to Third Sister all she heard.

One day, (23 March, 1940) word spread in the village that Lu-seng, Ma-pa and Ma-ma had returned and that if you wanted to hear Ma-pa preach you should come on Sunday noon.

That Sunday was a beautiful, quiet, sunny day, the peach blossoms shining pink against the new green of the mountainside, and as little Third Sister sat at her weaving, the music of happy hymns came floating down the slope to her. There was a new song, "When I see the Blood, I will pass over you." Whatever did those words mean? But oh, the lilting tune seemed to call to her. Years later, in giving her testimony, she told of it. "On Sunday I heard the lovely singing in the chapel and started up the hill, but had not the courage and turned back. That night, however, I slipped in, and I remember that Tychicus and I both took a stand for Christ then." Incidentally, Ma-ma's diary of that evening adds an interesting side-light. It says: "Lu-seng spoke so well to-night and on short notice."

So it was Lu-seng again! In God's hand he was the pickaxe that was loosing this little Lisu opal from its clinging earth. Third Sister was not yet born from above. Her testimony

continues: "I went on being a Christian but very carelessly."
Heathen Lisu, when annoyed, are foul of speech, and every
child learns those words as they grow up in the heathen atmosphere. It was with her tongue that Third Sister was careless,
but now she had an ideal shining in her heart. The noble face
of Lu-seng, with the light of heaven playing on it when he
preached, was an influence which unconsciously began to guard
the little girl from the mire into which other heathen of her age
commonly fall. All through the spring and summer months,
while working in the fields with young heathen companions,
Third Sister was "kept". When a young man would playfully
catch her by the arm, something within rose up and resented it.
All unconsciously this little stone of fire was beginning to learn,
"passion held by principle".

The end of August brought exciting news. Teacher Thomas,
his wife Homay, and their baby son John were coming to
Olives to be the Lisu pastor and family. What rejoicing among
the believers! For seven years there had been Christians in this
village, but never had they had a pastor of their own. Thomas
was to live in Lu-seng's guest-house, but it was so rickety that
it must be reinforced and the clay earth stamped down hard for
a smooth floor. What day could everybody help? The little
family were due to arrive on September 2nd so the place must
be in order by then. Much water would be needed to pour on
the floor before the earth could be stamped level and harden
well. The girls could carry the water. Homay had cooked for
the American missionary, so she was almost like a Chinese in
her clean-living habits, and she would like an earthen stove
instead of the Lisu iron tripod straddling a fire on the floor.
Well, clever-fingered Lu-seng-pa could make that, if some
of the young people would dig clay and the others carry it to
him. So a day was set and merrily the young group met, apportioned off jobs and worked together. Teasing, laughter and
witty repartee spiced the work (Jonathan and Tychicus were
such wags and Lu-seng-pa was the worst tease of all), so by the
set time the small home was ready, clean and neat with its hard
earth floor almost like cement, and all done by free, loving
labour.

Two or three days earlier some volunteers must go off to Oak Flat to help carry Homay's luggage. Incidentally, they would see and hear the closing day exercises of the Rainy Season Bible School—Lu-seng was one of the class speakers that year. How Third Sister would like to have gone, but the idea of a day's journey away from home was rather terrifying. No, she would stay and help get the Welcome Arch ready. She knew where some wild orchids grew in an old dead tree and they would look so pretty among the greenery of the arch.

All day her heart beat high with expectancy. Being a Christian brought so much new interest into life. The heathen said it was a dull existence without drinking whisky or smoking or singing the Try-to-Say-It,[1] but they just did not know. "The blessing of the Lord it maketh rich and he addeth no sorrow with it." Third Sister had seen the sorrows after a heathen night of carousing, knife wounds and brutal bruises; but the sweet blessing of preparing a home for your very own pastor, and meetings every evening such as the one they expected to have to-night! Lu-seng would be back and he would be sure to have new songs learned at the Bible School which had just closed. The Western reader, accustomed to all the fanfare of modern excitements, the wireless programmes, the flash of neon lights on highways, the ever-new magazine or book, cannot be expected to understand the delight and thrill of the simple children of the hills when a newly translated song or anthem is given to them. To them it is excitement, something new to break the monotony of the tedious daily round, and withal a new channel in which to praise God. They have no books, no shop windows in which to gaze and see a new thing, no news flashes of what the rest of the world is doing, no car or bicycle to take them to a change of scene. Life is very drab and laborious; but a new song stimulates new effort (for everybody learns each of the four parts by memory) and lends occasion for comment on unmelodious altos or straining tenors which usually ends in laughter. All over the world, get a group of young people together with something to do and you have—the spice of life. A new song is something to do!

[1] Heathen songs explained in *Nests Above the Abyss*.

About half-past four that afternoon the deep, mellow voice of a gong began to boom out over the hillside. It proclaimed that the travellers now sighted on the trail that circles such a long time before it enters the village would soon be at the welcome arch, where everyone must now gather. Down the mountain side and across the village trails they came running, and by the time Thomas' party had reached the arch, all the Christians were assembled on the other side of it. Manoah pitched the note, the four-part singers fell into harmony, and they all began to sing:

> *"There's a Teacher at the door,*
> *Let him in.*
> *He will teach us God's road,*
> *Let him in.*
> *That we might have salvation,*
> *That we might get to heaven*
> *God has given him to us,*
> *Let him in."*

When the song was finished, the guests passed under the arch and shook hands with the singers. Then all turned together to escort the little family up the hill to their new home.

Chapel was full that night. How everybody enjoyed it! That new tune to *Guide me, O Thou great Jehovah* was so winsome, it tied itself to your heartstrings and pulled a little.

> *Care and doubting, gloom and sorrow,*
> *Fear and shame are mine no more;*
> *Faith knows naught of dark tomorrow,*
> *For my Saviour goes before . . .*

and the Lisu version repeats it softly, "For my Saviour goes before."

Village of the Olives having sent four boys to study at Rainy Season Bible School this time, each must give a testimony—Thomas, Enoch, Jonah and Lu-seng. One of them mentioned that a world war had begun, and that Ma-ma had said that all should pray about it every week in the Saturday night prayer meetings. A country called France had fallen and another country called Japan was fighting China. "What queer names," thought little Third Sister. "How could one remember such names, let alone pronounce them?" War? In the canyon that had been shooting with cross-bows and poisoned arrows mainly, but really Third Sister could not picture it very clearly. "Perhaps that France-place did not have poison for their arrow-tips and that is why they were beaten so quickly. Well, it is too bad but —what a good time we had tonight!"

And now study began in earnest. As Homay was ill and getting worse, Teacher Thomas could not visit the neighbouring villages as he had at first planned. But that meant that he would be free to teach in Olives every night! He had decided to begin teaching the four parts to "All hail, Emmanuel." Third Sister found it hard to watch the words, the notes of her particular part, and the time-beat all at the same time. But when after many efforts the four parts were sung together the harmony delighted everyone. And then the boys were so jolly. Sosthenes was a bit too daring. Third Sister was glad she was little so that she could hide behind the others. Sarah, Lydia and Rhoda—they were the popular ones and the ones most teased; but they always knew what to answer back, whereas neither Third Sister nor Second Sister was quick at repartee. But they were both working hard at the catechism now, for Thomas was planning a baptismal service and knowledge of the catechism was considered essential in those days.

Now listen to her own account, given in her testimony some years later and written down even as she spoke: "My mother had died, and during this time my father, a heathen, was opposed to my being a Christian. My older sister wanted to be catechized also, so we studied secretly, not letting father know until we both had passed and were accepted for baptism. But after that event something happened to me inside, a transformation. Before that I was careless and often wrong in my speech but after my baptism I knew that I was different. I dearly love the words in Hebrews 11:1. I have *proved* that faith is the substance of things hoped for, the conviction of things not seen. It *is* a substance—it produces things tangible and real. And *decision* is another very powerful thing. I have been impressed anew with that, this year."

The listeners did not know all that her heart meant by that last sentence, until years later. Now let us see how this child of a primitive remote mountain canyon discovered that faith is a *substance*.

2

Stones in His Pocket

"Any valuable gem must first be trimmed, cleared, or sawed into suitable shape and size, then cut into the desired form and finally polished."

DR. KANZ, gem expert to Tiffany & Co.

AND so the great Quarrier, finding this little stone of fire willing to leave her earthen bed, begins to trim and clear for lapidary work. It is a thrill to turn up the pages of encyclopædias and look at the photographs of some of the world's most famous gems as they were first found in their rock or native condition. Only the Master lapidary's eye could detect value in them. So with these tribespeople, only looking with Christ's eyes upon them can one see possibilities upon which He may work. In the pages ahead He is going to trim off some ignorance, wash off the mud of heathen customs so long accepted as part of life, clear off a bit of superstition and place them under the running water of constant danger so that spiritual slovenliness may be removed. He has finer work yet to do, but we must patiently go with Him through all His preparations.

All that autumn, each evening, the small group at Olives met in their chapel. At first Homay tried to come also. She, so gifted and intelligent, could teach any part of any hymn, and not only knew as much Bible as her husband, but was also as good a writer. To find a Lisu girl equal in scholarship to any man in the church astonished Third Sister. The Lisu heathen always sneeringly said that women could not learn anything. Looking at Homay, Third Sister realized now that obviously this was not true. So gradually all her spare time was given up to reading her New Testament, memorizing Bible verses and going over her soprano part in the anthem they were attempting to learn—

"Lift up your heads, O ye gates, and the King of Glory shall come in!"

They meant to sing this at Christmas, but before that day arrived, something else—terrifying, thrilling, ominous—took place. Thomas had been teaching them 1 Thess. 4:13–19: "For the Lord himself shall descend from heaven with a shout . . . we shall be caught up . . . to meet the Lord in the air." Even the heathen heard of this wonderful expectation which Christians had.

It was a cloudy day and Third Sister was out on the mountains herding the family cows. Suddenly out of the sky came a great purring noise. She looked up but could see nothing—yet the noise continued. It seemed to be moving west. It was not thunder, it was a sort of purr, but no cat on earth could purr so loud—and how could a cat get up there? A few minutes and it was gone—silence. "The last trump." Could it be? Had the Lord come . . . *and left her*? Terrified she began to run hither and yon to collect the cows and drive them home. On the way she met another Christian carrying firewood—oh, what a relief it was! Then it was not the Lord's coming, for this Christian was still here.

"Did you hear a great noise out of the sky?" she called out.

"Yes," was the answer.

"What was it?"

"Don't know. Let's go home and ask."

So the two frightened little girls sped over the long, winding trail into Olives. Everywhere people were talking about it, but no one knew what it was.

That evening the little group in chapel anxiously inquired of Teacher Thomas. But even he did not know. "I thought maybe the Lord had come," he said simply.

"So did we!" sounded from many.

"So did Ju-shwey!" laughed Enoch. "He came running up to me and threw his arms round my neck and held on and yelled, 'If He takes you, He's got to take me too!' Say, I could hardly push him off, he hung on so. But when the noise went away he disappeared too."

How everybody laughed, for Ju-shwey was a backslider.

There were some more laughs and sly looks, for other backsliders had decided to repent that afternoon and were now in chapel—the first time for months.

The next afternoon about the same time the purr from the sky came again. "It's a tiger-demon!" declared the heathen, but this day there were no clouds and they *saw* it. It was moving across the sky. It had wings like a bird, only they did not go up and down, and a tail like a fish, and it purred like a tiger. Whatever could it be? Everyone in Lisuland had dropped his work and stood with open mouths gazing into the skies.

Only Teacher Thomas guessed aright. "I guess it's the Flying House that Ma-pa told us of!" he said with shining eyes. "People are inside it, but I don't know much about it. Wish I'd asked him more now!" Those were the first two planes to fly over the Hump; but from then on, as long as the war with Japan lasted, Flying Houses were of daily occurrence.

Christmas was near and everyone wanted to go to Oak Flat village so they could ask and hear about the Flying House. How did it get up there? Could it come down again? How did it find its way?—there are no trails in the sky. Could it go at night? Later they saw planes flying at night with green and red lights on their wings. "Really these white men are wonderful, there is nothing they cannot think up and do," they confided to one another.

That Christmas was Third Sister's first long trip away from home. She and Second Sister each had a new navy-blue homespun dress, woven and sewn by themselves, and a new bookbag with dainty embroidery at the edges, and cloth sandals embroidered with white. They had to carry their sleeping blanket and their food. Each must bring a quart of rice or corn, a pound of pork and a few ounces of salt for the feast.

Lu-seng had gone on ahead a day early, but Lu-seng-ma was going and Third Sister could stay close to her. Lu-seng-ma was very popular with the girls that year, and wise mother that she was, she knew why, but never let it be known that she did. She was anxious for a daughter-in-law because a daughter-in-law would give free labour on the farm and in weaving. Lu-seng was an only child now, since her two older ones had died, and no nice girl would come near their shanty for fear of gossip, since two eligible young men were there. Now that Lu-seng had taken to Bible study and preaching, they had to hire his cousin Timothy to herd the cows, gather firewood and help with the farm chores. Life is hard in the mountains.

Arrival at the river brink drove off all but happy thoughts. They had to wait their turn until the ferry boat arrived. At Olives they had a raft for crossing the Salween, and one sank to one's ankles in water. This plank rowboat was a veritable *Queen Mary* in Third Sister's eyes. While waiting for the current to swing the boat down to them, those who had brought lunches of cold boiled rice, ate them, and the boys showed their skill in stone-throwing. To be able to throw a stone across the Salween was an accomplishment. Lu-seng had done it, his mother declared proudly, which put the fellows on their mettle, and Sosthenes and one or two others made their stones "tang" on the rocks of the opposite shore to prove they were not far behind him.

Then with yells and shouts the ferrymen threw out their long hook and moored the boat up to the shore. Even so the crossing was formidable. When that swift mid-stream current caught the ferry it trembled from bow to stern like a frightened little bird, and was about as helpless. Third Sister having heard of the times this ferry had capsized and all on board were drowned, she and the girls cowered down, while Sosthenes grabbed hold of the oar and threw his powerful weight on it till it shot down on the eastern bank and, with shouts and cries, was safely hooked to the shore. Then did not he tease and pretend by terrified grimaces that "this was how Third Sister had looked", until the whole merry party was in fits of laughter!

Once over on the east bank, the little group took the small trail up to the road a thousand feet above their heads. That path is very steep, quite comparable to an attic staircase, but the only alternative would be the horse trail which hair-pins back and forth in a long detour of at least an hour's travelling. There was not even debate in their minds which to take, the steep thousand feet would not be as wearying as the long detour; so up, up through wild brush, and a cornfield here and there, digging their bare toes into the soil for a firmer foothold, they ascended. It was like a fly climbing a monstrous pail, for all above their heads towered mountain peaks, snow-crested, with just a bit of blue sky showing at the top. A thousand-foot hill is a mere bump in that country.

Up at the roadside they all threw themselves down for a delicious stretch and relaxation. The canyon opened up more fully from here, and they could see Sandalwood Flat village clinging to slopes higher than they on the mountains of the opposite bank. Turning their heads, they could see Golden Bamboo village like a platter on end, sprawling over the mountain to their right and at least five hundred feet higher than they. Sosthenes narrowed his eyes to gaze at the dipping, disappearing trail in an effort to discern if any of the Golden Bamboo Christians were in sight—a group must certainly be coming for Christmas. But not perceiving any, he turned to his lazy comrades and cried, "Up with you! The sun is already high and we do not want to be the last to arrive!" With good-natured talk and laughter, the others arose and were soon speeding along the trail south to Oak Flat.

Arriving at the last ascent, up on the rocks above their heads was perched the lookout man, and soon "bang-bang" went a gun. Third Sister winced. She had heard of those white-man weapons, but did not enjoy being so close. This time, however, she was careful to keep her fears from Sosthenes' sharp eyes. But here was Lu-seng, running down the trail to meet them, shaking hands with each, talking to everyone as he did so.

"I've arranged for you girls to sleep in Ma-ma's own house," he said. "You follow me as soon as we are through the welcome arch and I'll show you where to leave your things. We fellows will sleep in the servants' quarters." So saying, they arrived at the arch and lined up to be welcomed by song.

As Third Sister went down the reception committee line, shaking hands, she noted a new form. There was a new white Ma-pa! Oh yes, she remembered now, Lu-seng had said a new missionary had come[1]—Brother Five, they were to call him. How big he was—like Ma-pa himself. Of course he did not

[1] Orville Carlson.

know how to speak Lisu yet. Oh, here was Brother Three[1]
—always so kind, especially to women and children.

So this little village was Oak Flat! But *ah beh, ah beh*, look
how many Lisu were here, hundreds of them, running up and
down, chatting, staring, playing. Third Sister felt shy and
afraid for just one moment, then a tall strong form was at her
side and Lu-seng's comforting voice calmed her. "This way,
Olive villagers, as I told you!" And so, huddling up close to
the familiar figures of her own home-town folk, the little girl
found herself in House of Grace, in a side room away from the
multitude.

"At Christmas time everyone sleeps on the floor here," said
Lu-seng. "It's clean. Ma-ma washes it every few days." She
washes her *floor*! The girls looked at one another. How fussy
these white people were. Lisu floors were generations old and
had never been washed since they were laid. . . . Oh, what a
lovely sound! It must be the noise-box—let's go and listen.
And so the fun went on.

But something happened which nearly spoiled it all. Villagers
of Olives were all together in a side room, on the third evening,
singing their anthem together, when Lu-seng entered looking
hot and worried. He came close and spoke in a whisper that
stilled everyone immediately. "You girls go right away to bed
in Ma-ma's house, and all keep *close* together to-morrow morning
as you leave for home. This afternoon, while the open-air service
was on, some heathen fellows were up on the ridge watching.
Second son of the Tea family saw Second Sister here and liked
her. He has offered fifty dollars to each of his crowd if they will
help kidnap her to-morrow on the way home. He says he is
going to marry her by force."

Second Sister's lovely dark eyes dilated with fear even while
a flush of pleasure mounted to her forehead. To be selected from
eight hundred Lisu as the prettiest one—that was a compliment
to make anyone blush. But a forced marriage to a heathen—
Oh, the Lord deliver her! The next moment her face was so
scarlet she had to hide it behind tall Sarah, for the young men
from Olives were storming with wrath. "Steal one of our girls

[1] Charles Peterson.

when we fellows are about? Just let them try it!" In another moment heads were put together as they planned a guard on the journey home, who should go first and who should go last, until Second Sister was too embarrassed to stay. "Let's go to bed," she whispered, and like a flock of frightened sheep the girls, huddling together, scampered over to Ma-ma's house, into the side room, and tight-barred the door.

And now while they fall asleep, blessings of the Christmas message and excitement of this new occurrence alternately filling their thoughts, a word as to the family history of these two sisters.

That beauty should have been found in them was no surprise. Their mother had been a noted beauty and had fallen into the temptations which went with it. She had been married by her family to a man who was a stammerer, an affliction made more heavy by the fact that he was a very insipid character. Such a woman could never have loved such a man, and though divorce was too expensive to be contemplated there was the usual heathen way out. It was whispered in the village that Father Jiu was not the real father of any of his four children. First Sister had been so attractive that the feudal laird asked for her as his concubine. The payment was that Father Jiu would be forever exempted from government taxes of all kinds, and it is a revelation of his lack of character that he was quite pleased with the arrangement. But First Sister had lived only a year after that, and the laird himself died in 1942. His son, of whom we shall hear a great deal in the pages ahead, inherited his father's office and lands, but still there was tacit understanding that the Jiu family did not pay taxes. Such is the mire from which the great Master lapidary was planning to make jewels for his crown.

*   *   *

24 January 1941, Chinese New Year, and a new kind of danger.

In the mountains of the Salween canyon there are sulphur springs and the Lisu have discovered that it produces health to bathe in them. So, for who knows how many centuries, it has been the custom at Chinese New Year, the one general holiday time, to flock down from their mountain top homes to these several hot springs by the river side, and there, to bathe and carouse. Wine flows freely, bold licentious talk and ribald laughter fill the air, utterly strange young men make free with the girls and it is no place for a Christian. But Lisuland having no fairs or amusement parks, the excitement of the Hot Springs festival has a tremendous pull.

This particular year Lu-seng was told that Second Sister and some others, not strong in the faith, were planning to go. Immediately he called the deacons together to discuss what they could offer their Christian young people for that particular week, to counteract this attraction of Satan's? There is not much choice in Lisuland; a Bible study week with some new interesting song—could Ma-ma come and teach them? Unfortunately, she was not free, she replied. Nor could Ma-pa or Brother Three come, both were already promised elsewhere, but the new missionary, Brother Five, might come. He was only learning to speak Lisu as yet, but he spoke Chinese well. Gaius could come down from Sandalwood Flat village and interpret for him. Brother Five said he would be glad to come. And so it was arranged; two Olives boys went to carry Brother Five's bedding, an arch was built and on the appointed day the tall young Canadian missionary was sung through and under it.

A new white missionary is always of interest, but this one had brought an Hawaian guitar with him and a new song that Ma-ma had composed for the occasion. "O friend, come to the church on the mountains!" Brother Five had been a quartette singer at home, and second tenor was a new harmony to Lisu ears. So after he had taught them the soprano (new missionaries can learn to read Lisu long before they understand what they are reading) while they were singing he accompanied them on the guitar and sang second tenor. The lovely sighing of the instrument and the missionary's voice soaring over theirs, "Come, come, come, come,"—well, Second Sister and the others forgot all about the Hot Springs and attended every meeting.

At the end of the week it was hard to say which had enjoyed the time together more—Brother Five or the young people of Olives! They had been mutually blessed.

Ma-ma was eagerly awaiting the report of how things were going over on the west bank.

"We had a wonderful time!" the young missionary said enthusiastically. "Aren't they a grand bunch? They enjoyed the Bible study and quite fell in love with the song—they have the four parts memorized and are singing it everywhere. I heard it from a cornfield far down the mountain on the way home. And can't they pray! Those girls. . . ."

"But the girls don't pray," interrupted Ma-ma. "That has been our big trouble over there. Last year they just dissolved into giggles at the very idea of praying in public!"

"Well they do not now. Lu-seng and Jonah are very strict as to conduct in chapel and I did not hear any giggling in prayer time. Quite a few stood up each day and prayed. The news that the Japanese have bombed Paoshan[1] brings the war closer to home. The girls are praying, I can assure you."

And so this crisis passed, and the little stones down in His deep pocket had felt again the sweetness of the touch of His Hand.

*   *   *

It was May when another "keeping" took place. A hot afternoon was in prospect, the sun had risen high in a cloudless sky when there was a terrible roar and the earth shook until the pots all rattled. All afternoon ominous rumbles and belches of smoke to north and south alarmed them, and that evening when the little group gathered in chapel there were stories to hear. One of the boys had been visiting Sandalwood Flat (a Christian village the first mountain to the south of Olives). There had been a mighty landslide there. "I was on the trail about to start home," he said. "There was a fellow hoeing a field about five hundred feet beneath us. A huge slice of our mountain shot off when the earth quaked. We yelled, but there was not time. We saw the fellow throw up his arms as if calling for help and then he was buried alive. You couldn't dig him out; just about a whole ridge is on top of him, and the earth is still loose and sliding. There is a big crack in the Crown Rock at Sandalwood and there

[1] Paoshan is the Lisu missionary's supply base.

are rumbles coming out of it and smoke coming all the time. What is inside the mountain that could smoke? Does anyone know?" No, no one knew. The heathen say an earthquake is caused by a dragon inside the mountain turning over. But where was Lu-seng? . . . Lu-seng was out preaching . . . He was due to be on the road coming home . . .? Then oh, what a chorus of praises ascended to God when Lu-seng walked into chapel, safe and sound. He had much to tell; he estimated some forty had been killed up north, but not one Christian. Stories of the earthquake kept coming in for some days. The heathen said, "It is God's judgment on us for our sins"; and opportunities for preaching were excellent.

*　　　*　　　*

But soon another danger swept that one from memory. Last winter an order had come, compelling all in the canyon to plant opium. That did not concern Third Sister much because their fields were so low in altitude that opium could not thrive; the officials know that and automatically exempt them. But the Lisu Church? It was against the church rules to plant or trade or have anything to do with opium. So the Christians just refused the opium seed and planted wheat or potatoes as usual. But now an Opium Commissioner had appeared at Luchang, the county seat, to collect a tax on the opium and the laird was trying to collect the tax from the Christians too, even though they had not planted. Ma-pa was away on a trip, but Brother Three sent Lu-seng to call the deacons over to a consultation meeting at Oak Flat. How anxiously the little group at Olives prayed in the evenings and awaited the return of their deacons, Boanerges and Jonathan. Rainy Season Bible School had already started, and this year five of their boys were over there at Oak Flat studying—Lu-seng, Manoah, Gideon, Enoch and Jason. Thomas could not go yet, because Homay was very ill.

The situation had become more serious, since the official was threatening to drive off the cattle of any Christians who did not pay. At last Monday evening arrived and Boanerges stood up to give their report. The deacons from all over the canyon had met and decided three things. Firstly, to pay the tax if necessary, but on no account to plant opium. Secondly, to ask Ma-ma to write a letter of appeal to the President of China in the name of the Lisu church. The President was supposed to be a Christian, so if he said to pay they would do so, but their own opinion was that he knew nothing of this. Thirdly, to call the whole Lisu church to a day of fasting and prayer on June 8th. They had a good meeting, were all of one heart in the matter, and the Rainy Season Bible School was the largest yet, over forty enrolled, two of them coming from far away Goomoo in Burma!

How the tongues flew that night. Everyone was excited and thrilled. Everyone had the full confidence that the President would put an end to this persecution. June 8th was the next Sunday. All right. But how did one go about fasting and praying for a whole day, anyway? And so they discussed it long into the night.

Before Sunday, however, another matter had to occupy their thoughts. That Friday the suffering little Lisu Ma-ma had entered into peace. Third Sister was hardly out of bed when she heard the funeral song being sung up the mountainside: "When Jesus returns we shall meet again." Quickly she ran up the trail to Thomas' shanty; it was full of Christians, wet-eyed but quiet. Lu-seng-pa was getting out his own coffin and the deacons were discussing a place for the grave. In that primitive land where there are no undertakers or coffin merchants a death anywhere involves the whole village where it occurs. For this reason wealthy people get their coffins made ahead of time, and often have their graves dug also. (One old deacon in another village takes great pleasure in passing his own empty grave each Sunday on the way to church and complacently points out to his friends the Bible verse he has had written in black on its white-washed front!) So it was generous of Lu-seng-pa to offer his own coffin, for it would have taken days to make one.

Third Sister pushed past into the house. Thomas was there, his eyes red and swollen, baby John tied on his back. Homay lay in peace. She was so wasted she seemed to have shrunk to a child's size, but her face was serene. Third Sister's tears overflowed and Lu-seng-ma was crying unashamed. "She was only thirty," she murmured. "She had not lived her days to the full, not to the full!"

But there was much to do. The grave must be dug, then granite slabs chiselled out of the cliff to cover the coffin-hole and a pig killed to feed the workers. Everyone helps, of course, and their only wage is a free meal. The girls could help pound rice or corn, cook it and carry water, so Third Sister slipped back home and made arrangements with her father to be set free for that one day, in order to do her share. By night time all was finished and the dear one laid away.

Thomas was now free to proceed to Rainy Season Bible School. Lu-seng-ma offered to care for little John, but Thomas shook his head. "Thank you; not now. He is all I have left and I cannot bear to lose him right away." So with his baby on his back, the next morning the young father left for Oak Flat, and the little group at Olives said sadly to one another, "Will we never again have a teacher every night in the week?" "Let's meet, anyway. I'm coming every night," said Third Sister, instinctively feeling that Lu-seng would have it so. "I'll come too," said this one, then that one, and so the young group kept together.

One thing was eagerly anticipated. At communion week-end (the first Sunday in each month) there would be some Rainy Season Bible students come and speak to them and maybe this next time it would be Lu-seng! It was. Oh the meetings were always so good when Lu-seng led! He said he was proud of them that they had not given up their nightly meetings just because they did not have a teacher, and he drew up a schedule for them of writing, reading, conducting and sing-ing that they could study together. Third Sister's heart sung with joy and she inwardly vowed that she would never miss a meeting unless she was sick—a vow which she kept all her days. Even though Lu-seng had to leave again on Monday, he had been like a cool breeze on a hot, muggy day; you felt as if you had received new life to go on. And so the summer passed.

Every now and again the opium affair had come up, for it was far from settled. On July 27th came word that 140 Chinese soldiers had arrived at Luchang. Some said they were to fight the

Japanese; others whispered that they had come to compel the Christians to plant opium this autumn. On August 10th another big deacons' meeting was called. No answer had been received from the President and the Chinese official was getting angry—he said that Gaius of Sandalwood Flat was to pay fifty dollars for delaying like this. The Christians unitedly refused to pay until they had had the President's reply. "If he says we are to pay we will," they said in their simplicity, not realizing how it infuriated the Chinese to hear them link that great personage with their ragged selves—just as if there was any connection! But on August 26 word went swiftly over the canyon that Ma-ma had had an answer from the President's office and Lu-seng quickly typed out a translation and a copy was sent to each village. It said that the President had long been interested in the tribes and that he was glad there were missionaries ministering to them. As for the opium order, it was a mistake, and he was telegraphing the Provincial Governor about it immediately.

The church was jubilant. For the first time in all these centuries they had found someone to whom they could appeal for justice —someone higher in authority than the feudal laird or Chinese magistrate. It was just in time too, for the official was getting dangerous. He had laid hands on Acquila, the deacon at Sandalwood, had beaten and put him in prison and he was threatening to wipe out the whole of Plum Tree village and all its inhabitants! He had those 140 soldiers with guns now, and he had said that he would drive Ma-ma out of the canyon. If only Ma-pa would come back!

He did return, and on September 8th, together with a group of deacons, they went to expostulate with the feudal laird and the Chinese magistrate. The laird was nice, but fateful. "I'm sorry, Mr. Kuhn," he said, "I have orders from the Opium Commissioner, Chao Wei-yuen, to collect so much money from my district, and the only people in my district now that have any money are the Christians! The heathen are opium sots —they have not got such a sum. Yes, go on to Luchang and see the Chinese magistrate. If he lessens the tax, I will, of course."

At Luchang the official was courteous, made some vague promises and dismissed Ma-pa and the deacons and—Acquila was left in prison. Ma-pa then came on to Olives (Lu-seng was with him), and Third Sister had another gloriously happy week-end, a long one from Thursday to Tuesday. But the churches were puzzled. Why didn't the officials listen to Ma-pa and the President's instruction? One thing was clear—this opium-planting order was not from the Central Government. This local order was from the son of the Governor of the province, who meant to make private gain from it and considered the canyon too back-of-beyond for the President to hear of it. The Lisu church's appeal over his head had taken away his face, and he was furious.

On September 26th Ma-pa received a letter from a sub-official saying that he (Ma-pa) was to be made personally responsible for the church not planting opium! Then the very next day everyone was swung down to the depths of fear and despair. Ma-ma is a Canadian and her British Consul had written her a letter of stern rebuke for helping the Lisu church appeal to the President. "You should never have sent any letter except through me. You had no right to get mixed up in what is a purely political matter. You have forgotten that the canyon is border territory and you should be doubly careful. You were allowed in the canyon by the Chinese Government as a guest on the understanding that you take no part in politics, being there for religious purposes only. If they wish to carry out their threat to drive you from the canyon, I cannot help you. In fact, I must report you to the British Consul-General. The President will, of course, send a manifesto that opium-planting is not allowed, but it is doubtful if his *power* can reach to such a remote spot—in other words, whether or not the manifesto will be followed remains to be seen."

Even before word of this letter to Ma-ma reached Olives, one of their number came back from Luchang with the news that a new manifesto from the President had just arrived and was posted. But to everyone's puzzlement it read, "Anyone caught stealing will be executed." And the word "stealing" had obviously been pasted over the original words "planting opium". The local officials had won, and done just what the British Consul had prophesied.

There followed dark days as the little church swung back and forth from faith to fear, from fear to faith. The Chinese were jeering: now the church was going to be persecuted as never before! The governor's son had called all the officials out of the canyon for a big conference as to what should be done with those rebels, the Christians! Acquila was still in prison and some of the northern Christians had had their cattle driven off because they refused to pay until the President's answer arrived. And they had had their day of fasting and prayer, and it had availed nothing.

Does prayer avail nothing? "Faith is the evidence of things not seen" was Third Sister's favourite Bible verse. Away off in America, England and Australia, prayer helpers, although unseen, were already at work. "For thus saith the Lord, Ye shall not see wind, neither shall ye see rain; yet that valley shall be filled with water." (2 Kings 3:17). It was really so wonderful that we must share some inner details with you.

One afternoon Brother Three and Ma-ma were praying about the matter. From where they sat on the in-built veranda of the shanty they looked out upon the wonderful panorama of the Salween canyon. The mountain descends in bumpy ridges two thousand feet from the shanty at Oak Flat to the Salween River, and the opposite bank rises immediately for many thousand feet of foothills, knobs, ridges and peaks. Behind one small mountain crown, about level with Oak Flat in altitude, lies the magistrate's seat, the town of Luchang, where Acquila was in prison. As the two missionaries prayed, this petition was, as it were, forced from them: "Lord, do Thou Thyself *judge* these evil men who are inflicting such injustice upon Thy children."

That evening the Chinese magistrate and the Opium Commissioner were dining together. They began to quarrel. The Commissioner demanded the tax money; he could wait no longer. The magistrate replied he could not pay such a sum until the Christians paid. The Commissioner refused to believe it; made a sneering insinuation that the magistrate was trading illicitly with the Japanese over the pass. The argument became so hot that they fell upon one another physically. The Commissioner was a big man, the magistrate short and slender.

Fearful lest his son lose the fight, the magistrate's old father seized a knife and stabbed the Commissioner! He died on October 1st, 1941.

God had judged.

The magistrate was led out in chains after the coffin and—the whole affair fell into silence. On November 11th Acquila was quietly released from prison. On January 13th, 1942, the President's own men appeared in person on a tour of investigation up and down the canyon, and they personally supervised the up-rooting of all opium. The Christians had as yet paid out no money and the heathen lost their winter's crop—it was then too late to plant wheat or anything else.

The human explanation was never told. Ma-ma could only guess. Word came that the magistrate's only punishment was demotion. Her guess is, that to save his life he gave for the reason of their quarrel that he was backing up the President's manifesto, and thus won protection for himself from the highest power.

Yes, the running water of a constant peril washes away our slovenliness and alerts us to watch and pray. But the great Gem-Lover has compassion. Those anxious days how tenderly His fingers reached down into His mountain pocket and loved each touch of His trembling little stones of fire.

3

A Stone Selected

HOW did Heb. 11:1 become the favourite verse of a little uneducated tribesgirl, brought up in primitive fashion on the sides of a remote canyon at the end of the earth? This chapter holds the answer.

The year 1942 had dawned with a great hope. Ma-ma declared that she thought the time had now come to try a Bible school for girls! It could be only one month in duration, for the women in the canyon were much too busy to spare more time. And it must be at Chinese New Year, for only then had they any leisure. So it was planned for the month of February. Never had Third Sister heard of a school for girls only, and how her heart leaped in yearning at the thought. Oh that she might go! Second Sister had no such longings; and indeed, truth to tell, both sisters had started this new year badly. They had quarrelled, and then Third Sister's old heathen speech habits had rushed out on the end of her tongue. Second Sister had said that if Christians talked that way, then she did not want to be a Christian, and she had backslidden! It was really terrible, for that, of course, would bring the quarrel to Lu-seng's ears. Third Sister apologized humbly, but Second Sister was obdurate, intending Lu-seng to learn that she had backslidden because of Third Sister's angry words.

Lu-seng had gone to meet Ma-ma, who was coming that day to hold a short Bible study at Olives. Father, also angry at Third Sister, said that she might not go to the Bible classes —if she tried to, she could find her food elsewhere; he would give her nothing to eat. Also she might not go to the Girls' Bible School at Oak Flat. *That* was unthinkable. A Christian who got angry and fought with her sister was not worthy to go, and so on. When Third Sister could get alone on the wild mountainside, she threw herself on the grass and prayed in agony, "O Lord, I was wrong. I don't know why I did it. It just came out on my tongue before I knew it was there. Help me go to the Bible study this week!" While she prayed earnestly the golden sunshine poured down, yellow rock-primroses nodded their little heads by her side, and gradually a peace came into her heart and a resolution was formed. She would go to the Bible study and just not eat. Starving for two weeks did not kill a person; she remembered that Moses had been without food for forty days and forty nights! If it had to be a choice between spiritual food and physical, then she would choose the former. So with her mouth set firmly she arose, and ran down the mountain to resume her former task.

At 4.30 that afternoon gong! gong! gong! sounded over the mountainside announcing that Ma-ma and party were nearing the Welcome Arch. Third Sister came running along the lower trail and joined the line-up. Oh there was a Lisu Ma-ma along with the white woman—Esther from Stockade Hill! She wore the full skirt and short blouse of a Chinese, for the Lisu from near the Burma road were more civilized than those of the Upper Salween. After shaking hands, Third Sister shyly loosened Esther's bag, slinging it over her own small shoulder to carry up the hill, as the little group, chatting merrily, escorted the visitors up to Thomas' shanty, vacated now for Bible study time.

That evening Lu-seng spoke, while Third Sister shrank back into the shadowy parts of the chapel and listened, her whole soul open and drinking in every word. The Bible came alive to her when Lu-seng preached. She wondered if he had heard yet of the quarrel, and her eyes dropped while a flicker of pain passed over her face. He would be so disappointed. She prayed inwardly that she would be able to take his rebuke humbly. If necessary, she could prove that Second Sister was just as much in the wrong. But no, she had been wrong too. There was no excuse for having said angry words; she must pray daily about her tongue.

During Monday, Third Sister with firmly set mouth, went quietly through the day's study without anything to eat, not missing one class. It was two days later that Ma-ma learned of it, then she quickly called Lu-seng. "Do you know that there is a little girl studying with us who has had no food for a day and a half? Her heathen father said that if she came to classes he would not allow . . ."

"Yes, I know—just heard about it" said Lu-seng with a frown upon his usually sunny face. "Don't worry; she has been arranged for. Some of the other girls will feed her. But I cannot understand why people do not control their tongues better! There has been a quarrel in the village and one has backslidden because of the angry words of the other, who is a Christian." His handsome face was hot with indignation. Ma-ma watched him silently, a trace of amusement in her eyes. None was more hot tempered than Lu-seng himself! A most ardent nature, ardent in love and ardent in anger. It is true that heathen words were barred from his mouth, but his natural gift of speech was so eloquent he suffered nothing from their loss. He could barb his words most effectively without any help from the heathen vocabulary. Possibly there were others in the village with the same disposition? Ma-ma, quite ignorant who the culprits were, was not inclined to be upset over the matter.

"Well, we ought to go and exhort them," said Lu-seng. "We are busy to-day, but will you go with me on Saturday? Some are girls and I do not like to go alone."

"Oh certainly," said Ma-ma. "Gladly. Let us set aside Saturday for exhorting the unbelievers in this village, shall we?" And so it was arranged.

That Saturday was sunny and clear. The skies were such a deep blue where they could be discerned between the snowy summits, thousands of feet high, which pierced their depth on each bank of the canyon, and up whose sloping sides downy white clouds were travelling. Second Sister determined to weave that morning, and as she seated herself at the loom outside their hut she could see the mountain slopes opposite to Olives. A baby cloud was nestling in the curve of one giant peak, as if it had got lost in the long ascent and, weary of trying to find the top, had gone to sleep in the shelter of those massive crags. Everywhere the fresh green of new spring and the little keen nip which departing winter had left in the air stirred the blood into spring fever. Second Sister had just got her loom arranged and had begun to pedal it when Lu-seng and Ma-ma appeared in front of her. Third Sister hung anxiously and shyly in the shadow of the doorway. Lu-seng did the exhorting. Standing there with a slight frown on his face, he went right to the point.

"I was sorry to hear that you have backslidden, Second Sister. I've heard all about it. Third Sister was wrong to speak like that, but she says she is willing to apologize. And God says that he will not have compassion on those that 'will not from their hearts forgive every one his brother their trespasses'. Eternal life is not a toy to be taken up and tossed down from petulance. And God is not to be played with, walking with Him one moment and turning your back on Him the next!"

Second Sister's face was drooping. She looked very sweet and penitent and a bit scared. "I'm sorry. I was wrong," she murmured.

"Well, will you say you were wrong to Ma-ma here? And shake hands with her?"[1] Was it the sun in his face, or what was it—Lu-seng was scowling. But Ma-ma—Second Sister was not afraid of Ma-ma. She instantly stood up and held out her hand. "I was wrong. Forgive me," she said simply.

"And I'll expect to see you in chapel to-night" said Lu-seng, his face clearing. "And we'll give you an opportunity to stand up and confess to the brethren. And you too, Third Sister?" with a short nod to the shadowy form in the doorway. Then the little group passed on to another hut.

Third Sister came out from the door and put out her hand to Second Sister. "I'm glad you've come back. Please forgive me. I'll try never to say those bad things again."

Second Sister, with a mollified look, accepted the handshake. "Will you help me find the words I've got to say in chapel to-night?"

"Sure I will," said God's little Stone of Fire. "And I'll make my confession first. Then they'll understand and it will be easier for you." And that was the last quarrel between the sisters that Ma-ma ever heard of.

[1] In Lisuland shaking hands is not a token of friendship but a sign of being in church fellowship.

That Bible study week was a happy time. Lu-seng had so much fun and originality and everyone was on the *qui vive*. In the Lisu work there have been mass movements, whole families, even whole villages turning to Christianity at once. But Olives is different; they are hand-picked fruit. The greater majority of those attending these Bible classes were young people who had become Christians in defiance of their heathen parents' threats. The sense of common persecution knit them together and all were young and most of them unmarried. Ma-ma was very conscious of this latter fact since she had learned that Lu-seng had begun to build his own house. He would never own up to any such idea, and certainly showed no sign of favouritism among the girls but Ma-ma was learning to read Lisu actions. The missionaries had discovered, through sad experience, that it is a very important matter to whom a promising young evangelist proposes. More than one has been ruined for the Lord's work by choosing an unsuitable wife. So at free periods between classes, Ma-ma wondered vaguely which of the girls Lu-seng might have in mind. He himself would not discuss the matter, but there was the silent sign of his own house going up. The four girls most likely to be chosen were Rhoda, Lydia, Sarah or Second Sister. Of these four, tall pretty Sarah, bright of mind and spicy of tongue, seemed to gain ascendancy; for Lu-seng openly praised her abilities to answer the Bible questions, and when a Bible match was organized he chose Sarah first for his side, even before Esther herself! And he did not choose Third Sister at all.

Toward the end of the week Second Sister and Third Sister invited Ma-ma and Lu-seng to a supper prepared by themselves —rice and chicken. Lu-seng pretended he was too busy to come, but Third Sister quietly refused to escort the party down the hill until Lu-seng came. Ma-ma only now learned her name, but her face had been the biggest inspiration of that particular school. She sat on the front row among the sopranos, for in that village the whole audience is the choir, seated according to the part they sing! Third Sister seemed to open up her whole soul to the message and allowed the speaker to pour it in to the full. Also the sweet shyness that flooded her face when she noticed she had attracted attention bespoke a maiden modesty most winsome. But she also had a very determined jaw—there was obstinacy there, Ma-ma saw as Third Sister quietly refused to budge until Lu-seng had joined their party. But once he started with them, all was happy enjoyment.

The very next day, before the evening service, Lu-seng walked into Ma-ma's hut with the worried look that bespoke a problem. Knowing him well, Ma-ma asked what it was.

"Soldiers in the village to-night," he replied shortly. "It's not good for the girls. They shouldn't be seen on the trails and even in their own homes it is not good."

"But in their own homes won't their parents protect them?"

"What protection has a Lisu against a gun? These are Chinese soldiers, I've known them break down a barred door. To a heathen parent resistance is not worth that. Protection at that price is too dear—and most of our girls' parents are heathen, you know. They don't think sin is that important."

"Well, then, tell all the girls to come and sleep at my house to-night! I'd like to see those soldiers attempt to break down *my* door!" and Ma-ma bristled like an old hen with a dozen chicks to cover.

Lu-seng's face cleared. "All right. If they sleep on the floor, they can all get in!" And so the announcement was whispered all over the village, and chapel saw a full attendance that evening.

After a bright and happy service, Thomas' hut was a bevy of giggling laughing girls preparing to sleep sardine-fashion on the floor. Lu-seng came in, trying not to look as self-conscious as he felt.

"Everybody in?"

"All but Third Sister," came a chorus of girlish voices.

Third Sister? She lived at the very bottom of the village. Lu-seng turned and shot out into the dark. And after about three minutes the door opened and Third Sister entered flushed, and a lovely light of happiness on her face. As she stands there, the light from a wood fire on the floor playing over her form, let us take a look at her. She was short, because Lisu grow slowly, not maturing until they are twenty-five, and she was

just turning seventeen by our count, eighteen by theirs.[1] Large
dark eyes with a sharply curved eyebrow that gave a piquant
expression to her sweet face. When she smiled as now, she
showed the most beautiful even pearly teeth Ma-ma had ever
seen, and a delicate pink flush on her cheeks was most becoming.
However, the loveliest of all were shy gentle movements and
expressions that we call "charm," elusive to description and, sad
to say, never once captured by the camera. As she murmured
an explanation and quickly tried to slip out of sight, Ma-ma
said to herself, "You are the sweetest of them all. I wonder
Lu-seng hasn't got the sense to see it." But, remembering how
that high-strung young colt resented any feel of the bridle on
his neck, Ma-ma sighed and resorted to prayer.

The next afternoon's study was broken by a summons for
Ma-ma. "The soldiers" were the opium investigation committee sent by the President, and they wished to see Ma-ma.
The laird's son, his heir, was with them and the corporal of the
local militia, who was a relative of the laird's. The latter flung
out a finger at Ma-ma and said, "You're responsible for this!"
and Ma-ma knew she had made an enemy for life. Inwardly
she sighed and prayed, "Yea, Lord, I've learned my lesson.
Never again will I 'go down to Egypt' for help. Never again."

The next day Bible study was over and Ma-ma had to leave.
As she shook hands with Third Sister, Ma-ma said, "Third
Sister, don't you give up hope of going to Girls' Bible School
next month. God is able to open your way, and I will join you
in prayer about it."

"Thank you, Ma-ma," she replied simply. "God is the only
one who can. Father steadfastly refuses to let me."

"Don't let lack of board money keep you away, if your
father will consent. I'll see to the money," Ma-ma said earnestly.

"Thank you to death, Ma-ma," and then they had to
separate. The girls stood on a rock that juts out beside the road
and overlooks the trail ahead for a long distance, and they

[1] The Lisu reckon that a baby is a year old when it is born, and two
years old as soon as Chinese New Year comes. Thus a baby born in
December would be two years old by Chinese New Year, which is,
roughly speaking, about February 1st.

sang songs until Ma-ma and her carriers were out of sight.

Third Sister turned back to her old pursuits and her old life with just one purpose in her heart. She must get to the Girls' Bible School in February. Ma-ma had taught them the stories of Joshua during that Bible study. It was God, and God only, who had levelled the walls of Jericho. Her father's adamant refusal to let her go was like a city wall that only God could level, but she was going to walk around it in prayer every day—seven times a day if necessary!

And on the seventh day God levelled the walls.

It was a lovely sunny morning in January—Yunnan's loveliest month of the year. How blue are the skies, how warm the golden sunshine, how crisp the mountain air blowing from tall snowy peaks! It is probable that Third Sister was sitting at her loom, weaving by the side of their house—for all the girls who hoped to be free to go to Girls' Bible School had to work overtime to get the family weaving done in order to have a whole month free. Boanerges' tall form appeared beside the busy little weaver and his wrinkled face was wreathed in a broad grin. He looked quickly up and down to make sure no one was in sight, then he said in a low voice, "Here's a like-letter for you. You're not to tell anyone, but slip me the answer when I come round to-night." With a quizzical humorous twinkle in his eyes, he handed Third Sister a small folded square of paper; then he walked off.

Third Sister's heart stood still. Chinese New Year was just a few days off, when she would be considered eighteen years old; the Lisu church say a maiden may not be proposed to until she is eighteen, and the proposal is called a "like-letter". In the Lisu church, with its background of heathenism and loose speech, the boy may not propose in person. He must write a like-letter and hand it to the deacon of the village, who reads it to see if its language is what the church may approve, and then the deacon takes it to the girl. She, likewise, must write an answer through the deacon. On no account must they hand their letters to one another personally, and they are horrified at American customs in this matter and consider that we Westerners are sadly loose. Their joys are all the sweeter for waiting until marriage makes

them one in the Lord; divorce is unusual, and is still considered
a scandal.

Third Sister sat there with the small missive in her hand, as
if paralysed. She did not need to open it to know the writer's
name. Her little notebook of Christian Endeavour speeches was
full of outlines and texts written in that strong, bold handwriting. Lu-seng! How could it be? To *her*?

Her next emotion was terror, lest anyone should see. To open
and read it outside was too risky. Where could she fly for refuge?
Into their little shanty she ran hunting desperately. Maybe she
chose the far corner of the porch, where a huge grain bin
stands. If she squeezed in between that bin and the wall she
would never be detected. With trembling fingers, and eyes
with the guard down, her whole soul of love pouring through,
she opened Lu-seng's like-letter and read it. It called her "Sister".
Oh yes, she understood that. Lu-seng so feared heathen impu-
tations and innuendos that he would choose the purest name he
knew—and she loved him for it. It asked her to marry him in a
year or two, and not to be afraid or embarrassed to answer him.
He wanted it to be a holy union where the spiritual rather than
the physical predominated. But above all, this proposal was
based on one condition—that she promise never to interfere
in his Bible study or work for the Lord, which would of course
call him from home many weeks at a time and leave her to do
the farm work alone. On his part he promised always to see that
each year she was always free for the month of February to
attend the Girls' Bible School. They must covenant mutually to
protect one another's privilege of Bible study, for the old parents
would not be sympathetic. And it finished: "If you can't like
me, I'll die a single man." O Lu-seng, Lu-seng! You start with
such staid propriety, calling her "Sister," and end up like that!
But Lisu opals have fire at their hearts. "Principle shot through
with passion." Then did the tears of joy descend. And what a
day that was. Most surely the weaving loom stood idle. Most
surely the little brown hand shook so that page after page was
pronounced unfit to be sent, torn up and a new sheet pulled
eagerly forward for a new start. Ma-ma never got to see it,
but she was told its contents and the sweet winsome shyness

which later made Third Sister the like-letter scribe of her village.
Ma-ma read the answers Third Sister wrote for other trembling
maidens in later days, so let's try and imagine this, her first.

To Brother Lu-seng.
     If you can like such an immature, ignorant, inexperienced
little thing as I am, then—yes. In three or four years' time I
will be pleased to marry you. And I promise to do as you said
—always to help guard your call of God to preach and study
His word. I would be glad to do that—that's my heart too.
The writer is
                    Third Sister of the Jiu Family.
     PS.—Thank you very much.

That PS. is untranslatable. English does not possess a word
to tack on the end of "thank you", which has a coy, shy grateful
smile in it; but Lisu has. One thing is sure: that Lu-seng's heart
took a second tumble when he read it, and that he tossed back
his black curls and felt that the world was beneath his feet.
     But the happy little girl must come out of her hiding-place.
She must get the note to Boanerges. And her father must be
told. Would he give her to Lu-seng? How fast her heart beat.
If father married her to a heathen, he could get a lot of money
for her; the church refused to allow a "dowry"; he would get
nothing but a good son-in-law if he gave her to Lu-seng.
Would he consent? But even if he did not, to-day's joy was
enough—Lu-seng loved her even as she loved him. That was
happiness enough for many days to come.
     But how to keep it secret? She understood why he wanted
it kept secret. Because it would save them both words from
the heathen which bring a blush of shame. It must come sooner
or later, but if it came just before they would be married there
would be fewer days to endure it. But how to keep it secret?
Third Sister was afraid that the joy on her face alone would
proclaim it to all the world. And Second Sister? She felt sorry for
Second Sister. She would be as kind to her as she knew how.
That evening Third Sister waited until all were in chapel, then
she slipped in when the pine-chip light was waning and hid
behind the other girls. She saw Lu-seng searching the girls' side

with his eyes, but she deliberately hid. She could not trust her face in public if their eyes should meet; his anxiety would be short-lived: he would receive her reply to-night.

The next day Boanerges had to find Third Sister's father and tell him the news in secret, and that Lu-seng wished the engagement, if there was to be an engagement, kept quiet. Father Jiu consented, but had a great deal to say about how much money he lost by the transaction. He wanted Lu-seng to understand that he would not have done this for everybody, and that Lu-seng ought to be properly grateful. It was obvious to all that the old man was inwardly very proud that he was to have a son-in-law whom all the community prized.

But being a heathen, the first thing to do really, was to compare their horoscopes. Lu-seng was born in the year presided over by Goat, and Third Sister in the year presided over by Cow. Now this was alarming, for the Goat and the Cow are in opposition—they fight; in other words the horoscopes were unfavourable. Of course the Christians call that superstitious, but old Father Jiu was not a Christian. If the horoscopes were unfavourable, his daughter might die soon after marriage; he could not consent to that. Yet in his heart he was disquieted at the possibility of losing such a son-in-law. What should he do? If he allowed a union of opposing horoscopes he would offend the gods, and if he did not, he would lose an honour which would make him the envy of his neighbours. Suddenly an idea occurred to him.

"Boanerges, why not let Lu-seng take Second Sister instead? She was born in the Rabbit year. Goats and Rabbits don't fight."

Well, that was an idea, and the kind of thing the heathen did all the time: in other words, acceptable to Lisu thinking. Come to think of it, Lu-seng used to like Second Sister. Boanerges remembered how Lu-seng-pa had chuckled many years ago, when one evening his eight-year-old son returned home to supper and told the family that he had seen his future wife that day! He refused to give her name, but the amused parents by the process of elimination had discovered it was the Second Sister of the Jiu family! This story cheered Father Jiu immensely and

Boanerges was commissioned to go and suggest this way out of the difficulty. Too bad for Third Sister, but it was for her good, and Lu-seng would still be in the family.

Only God knows the agony of heart that little Third Sister went through all that day before the interview with Lu-seng could take place. A height of joy one day, and an agony of despair the next. O God, would you really let that happen? What was that Bible verse . . . "What man is there of you, whom if his son ask bread will he give him a stone? . . . How much more shall your Father which is in heaven give good things to them that ask Him?" That was something faith could lay hold of. "Faith is the conviction of things not seen." The conviction that the One not seen and silent is still working and true to His promises. All through that day Third Sister laid hold of that faith to still her trembling hands and fearful heart.

That evening as dusk fell, Boanerges entered the Jiu shack once more. Third Sister trembled so that she quickly moved into a dark corner of the hut so as not to be seen when sentence was given.

"It won't work," announced Boanerges. "It made Lu-seng so mad that even I got scared. I left as soon as possible. You should have seen his eyes flash. It's Third Sister or nobody *ever*, as long as he lives, he said. And he got so excited I felt as if I were sitting on gunpowder and the match had been lit. That boy is like his great-grandfather, and woe betide anyone who crossed his great-grandfather! I tell you, I got out as fast as I dared and I recommend you don't try that again. Or if you do"— and Boanerges chuckled—"go sit on the gunpowder yourself!"

You remember Father Jiu is a stammerer. For the next fifteen minutes' conversation could not have been clear. It takes him such a long time to get his first word out normally when he is excited that we can only imagine his "Bu-bu-bu-buts" at Boanerges' words. Even Third Sister, hiding in the corner and weak from relief, must have finally re-hid her face, this time to conceal the chuckles at her father's flounderings. He had really begun to count on having Lu-seng as his son-in-law, and now he had not only badly offended him, but had made an adjustment difficult by his strong declaration that the horoscopes were impossibly opposed! But Boanerges is a clever old man and he really wanted to help.

"There is one thing we have not done yet," he said. "We have only compared the years of their birth. Do you remember the animal presiding over the day Third Sister was born?" Lisu, who have never studied in their lives and cannot multiply or divide and must count on their fingers, never forget the horoscopes of their children. Yes, Father Jiu knew the Day Animal of Third Sister; so when the horoscopes of the two animals who presided over the day of their birth were compared, to everyone's relief they were found to be in harmony.

"If the day horoscopes are in accord, I would not worry about the year horoscopes," counselled wise Boanerges. "Lu-seng isn't afraid, and he knows a lot, that boy."

And so the engagement was made, and still in secret. The next day Boanerges appeared with two big tubes of delicious honey—the engagement present to the father. "And, of course," says Boanerges casually, "you will let Third Sister go to the Girls' Bible School now. Lu-seng requests that you do."

And so the walls of her Jericho fell. "Faith is the substance of things hoped for," she testified in later years with an earnest light on her sweet face. "It *is* a substance, something *real*."

4

Two Stones Are Set Together

AND now the building of Lu-seng's house went on apace.
It had been rumoured in the village that Lu-seng had
written a like-letter, but no one could find out to whom or
with what result; Boanerges could keep counsel.

The road to the water-hole passes right by and through Lu-
seng's property, so that Third Sister was daily able to watch
the progress of the building as she went for water. The new
home was not like any Lisu house ever seen in those parts before.
It was really a miniature copy of Ma-pa's House of Grace, with
three rooms instead of the Lisu one. That meant privacy for
the bride and groom, which must have thrilled Third Sister's
heart. Lu-seng-pa was one of the best carpenters in the canyon,
so it was being built well; it was to have windows in it, also
an innovation, because, being Bible students, they would need
light to study. It was *not* to have a central fire; it was to be
kept clean; they would cook and eat with the old parents,
whose house was already sooty.

Third Sister carefully avoided Lu-seng now. She was still
afraid of her tell-tale face; besides, avoidance was chaste etiquette
in the Lisu mind. She would see him every night in chapel and
it thrilled her through and through when night by night she
watched him search for her with his eyes until he found her, then
though he looked away immediately, his whole face lit up with
such a happy light she marvelled that no one else had discovered
their secret. And with what power he preached those evenings!
He just radiated the joy that was flooding them both. Always
before that, after chapel service, Third Sister had lingered with
the rest of the girls outside the door, talking back and forth
with the young men about the events of the day or the latest

news of the war. But now, as soon as it was over, Third Sister sped quickly down the trail to her father's house. She made the excuse that she had so much weaving to do now that she was going to Girls' Bible School and would lose that month.

But one day on the way up to the water-hole, her empty bamboo tubes in the basket on her back, Third Sister ran right into Lu-seng, who was coming back with his load of water. They were upon one another before they realized it, and the soul of Lu-seng leaped up into his face with such a glow of love that Third Sister was shyly overcome and sped up the hill and past him. Neither had said a word, but that night the little girl lay awake and under privacy of the darkness leisurely enjoyed it all over again. Those were happy days.

Five girls from Olives were going to Girls' Bible School— Sarah, Lydia, Chloe, Rachel and Third Sister. Lu-seng was journeying with them to get Ma-pa's white mules and take them over to Olives for winter pasture. Second Sister seemed to be backsliding again. She said she was going to the Hot Springs at Chinese New Year and Third Sister's heart was burdened for her.

The day of departure came, and the gay young party started out. Some of their brothers went along to help carry their bedding rolls, and as they passed along the trails and met boys who had been to the Rainy Season Bible School there was merry teasing.

"We'll expect you back in two days! Girls will get home-sick: you will never be able to stick it!"

"Be sure and bring an extra copy of the new songs for me, won't you?"

"You will have to go out on the week-ends and preach, you know! We'll have a special prayer for you!" and so on. The girls would laugh and blush and shake their heads, or give a call back, and so they left the dear, familiar village their hearts fluttering but eager, for it certainly started a new page in life for each.

This group from Olives were among the first to arrive, and Ma-ma met them, running down the trail to welcome them, in fact. When she came to Third Sister she exclaimed, "Why,

Third Sister! So you came after all, praise God," and she shook her hand in such surprise that Third Sister felt guilty—evidently Ma-ma herself did not know yet. But Lu-seng was already inspecting the two small dormitories and choosing the better.

"Here, girls, put your bundles in here. Yes," testing the woven bamboo mats tied to short posts driven into the earth, "these beds will do all right. Two in a bed—choose your partner. Maybe the fifth one of you can sleep with Esther." And so he went around arranging for their comfort.

That night after service Lu-seng told Ma-ma.

"You enigma!" said Ma-ma. "Here you led me to think that you were interested in Sarah, and I was so concerned, for your two temperaments would never have harmonized. Third Sister? I am delighted. She was my choice of them all. But you never showed the slightest interest in her?"

How Lu-seng laughed. How he threw back his black curls with a joyous toss as he said, "It wasn't convenient to let you know. And I don't want it known now! And I want to pay for her study books, please," as he laid two dollars on Ma-ma's knee.

Now Ma-ma knew that Lu-seng had very little spending money, so she said, "Oh I would be glad to pay for her."

"No; you do not understand. I *want* to," and his face glowed so unmistakably that Ma-ma understood.

"All right then. But I am giving the girls Bible names—those who do not have them. Wouldn't you like to choose Third Sister's?"

Once more his face beamed, then sobered as he thought. "The Lisu translation of girls' Bible names does not appeal to me—with one exception. Mary is a nice name."

"Then she shall be Mary," announced Ma-ma, and that is how Third Sister got her Bible name.

They wanted their engagement kept secret and Ma-ma really meant to help, but yet it was Ma-ma who unwittingly let the cat out of the bag, She was so busy that morning. Lu-seng was leaving with the mules, and the girls were all clamouring to buy notebooks and pencils, pens and ink. Not having the time to speak to Mary previously when that little maiden shyly produced a dollar, Ma-ma said to her, "You do not need to pay, Mary. One of the Christians in Olives is paying for you."

The idea of helping a Christian student through Bible School is such a common one in America, that it did not occur to Ma-ma a Lisu would never think of such a way of serving the Lord, and that by her remark she had publicly announced that the giver was Lu-seng! But so it was.

That afternoon Ma-ma called Mary aside. "Mary, would you like to join me each evening when I go for my prayer walk? We could pray together for Lu-seng; you know he is going to Stumpy Stream district to evangelize among the heathen this month. That is a difficult territory and he will need special upholding." Now Ma-ma had hoped to get to know her better through these times together, but the little girl was so in awe of the tall white woman that she did not speak a word except when asked a question. Her prayers for Lu-seng, however, were free and from the heart, showing that communion with the Father was not new to her.

It was on the playground, in after study time, that Ma-ma really learned to know her. If she made a mistake or caused others to lose a game, she was humble and very quick to ask pardon. And she loved her fellow villagers devotedly. At every prayer meeting, then and in succeeding years, she was always one of the first to pray and never closed without a yearning "and God bless the dear brothers and sisters in Olives." In her studies she did not top the list that year, but in later schools she did excellent work; and in the last school Ma-ma was able to teach in the canyon, Mary turned in a perfect paper in Ma-ma's subject, the whole month.

Closing day was thrilling. Lisuland saw its first line of twenty-four girl students take their places on the platform. Two girls gave short messages, and for the rest the programme was singing and Bible memory work. The possibility of the women of Lisuland teaching the children had been introduced, and to help them, some action songs were translated. These the girls did together, and being a new thing in Lisuland, made a great impression, even the adults enjoying them to the full. Many guests had arrived for the closing exercises, among them a contingent of young men from Olives. At the end as the girls marched out, Enoch said beaming, "Why, it was almost as good as *ours*, wasn't it?"

Ma-ma smiled and inwardly answered, "Masculine vanity. *I* think it was better!"

On their return to Olives, everyone was waiting to see what a month's Bible study had done for girls. So night by night the girls were summoned to the platform to teach what they had learned. Sarah had been impressed with a message on Joseph, on how the Lord had to deal with his youthful pride. Mary remembered a talk on the mother of Jesus and the danger of the daily round, the familiar task dulling the memory of the heavenly vision. And so on. And everyone enjoyed the action songs.

Only a few nights had passed when, lo and behold! Lu-seng arrived. He really had not planned to return so soon, but, of course, his imagination pictured what was going on; he wondered if Mary could preach in Christian Endeavour better now, and what new songs she had learned and so on until he found himself going home. He explained it to everyone by saying it was because he had torn his trousers and had had to come home to get them mended. But as he prepared to return to his field he wrote to Ma-ma, "They have all come back new girls!" And so the yearly Girls' Bible School came to stay.

Those were happy days for the young group, unconscious of the dark cloud of war that was slowly but surely gathering over their heads. Two more like-letters were written, Enoch to Sarah and Tychicus to Chloe. Jonah, the middle man, said to Ma-ma, "It is strange, but I noticed that Sarah's answer to Enoch was *written in Mary's handwriting*." And thus began her long role of village like-letter scribe. One is tempted to linger over the picture of those two maidens, in a hidden corner of the wooded mountainside, their turbaned heads together as they whispered and concocted that important small missive. Ma-ma saw it later. There had obviously been writings erased and on-second-thoughts put down in their place. It had a sweet, winsome note which betrayed the identity of the composer even more than the handwriting! But Enoch was satisfied and the engagement announced.

And now for those dark clouds. Ma-ma had gone to Kunming for dentistry and Ma-pa for another one of those conferences, but Brother Three and a friend were still in the canyon. Two months after Girls' Bible School the Japanese were at the China-Burma border. In May, without notice, they bombed the city of Paoshan at noon on a market day. The carnage was unspeakable, but in the Lord's loving-kindness the missionaries all escaped with their lives, and on May 9th five of them arrived at Oak Flat! This upsurge of war had blocked Ma-pa and Ma-ma's return, but here were all these refugee missionaries; so Rainy Season Bible School had plenty of white teachers. These new voices were much appreciated, but, of course, none of them spoke Lisu and prayer was made constantly that their own missionaries might return. God answered in an unexpected way. The Chinese military found that they needed a dependable liaison officer who understood the Lisu language and customs, and who would plead with the tribespeople not to befriend the Japanese. For this office Ma-pa was chosen; and Ma-ma with him, they were allowed in past the line of American soldiers (who were longing to get closer) and by the end of August were back in the canyon again. Lisuland was now considered the front line of battle, so it was like a miracle. They were learning what God can do when people pray.

But Mary's thoughts were not often on the war. Lu-seng had said in his proposal that they would be married in a year or two, and she had replied, "In three or four years", but now, she was told, he wished to be married that autumn! Fearful lest her heathen father change his mind, the date was set for November 13th. There was no trousseau to be prepared, but the clothes for New Year could be hastened on, and for Lu-seng a pair of cloth shoes. Like all other Lisu, he usually went barefoot. But from the Chinese, Village of the Olives girls had learned to make cloth shoes and beautifully embroidered sandals, which were the envy of other villagers. Lu-seng should have a pair of these. As little Mary was not especially good at sewing, she doubtless sought advice from clever-fingered Rhoda or Lydia.

From now on, according to native custom, the labour of making all Lu-seng's clothes would devolve upon his wife. So Mary, pleased with the prospect, as she had occasion to go back and forth through the village, secretly watched the married women cut out their men's clothes, hoping to get hints.

For about a month before the wedding Father Jiu had travelled north and south inviting his friends and relatives to the marriage. This important role he enjoyed to the full, for he was allowed to invite as many as he liked, and he intended that the guest-roll should be at least one hundred. If he gave away his daughter for nothing, at least there should be a properly expensive affair, and a good audience to witness his generosity. Lu-seng, of course, must feed them all. The only drawback to this proud joy was that he had to tell everybody that there would be no liquor served. These Christians—well, you know that is their custom. But Lu-seng says there will be plenty of rice and pork, enough to take some home with you—so bring a big square of cloth to wrap it in! Of course, wherever he went Father Jiu had to stay overnight, and we can imagine the covert laughter as the old stutterer tried to expatiate proudly on the beautiful new house which was to be his daughter's. There were sliding shutters for the windows, which, of course, were open, glass being an impossible luxury, and Lu-seng-pa had a plan to fasten them against thieves. The board floors were held down by nails; in fact, the whole house was built with nails instead of being tied together with vine in the usual Lisu manner. The nails were the wedding gift of Ma-pa, whilst Ma-ma's gift, two cupboards, were large enough to do duty as beds, as well as being containers. Father Jiu had lots to talk about. Lu-seng's desire for a large house was in order that church guests could have a good place to sleep both at Christmas time and for the present occasion. The wedding guests were to sleep on the new board floors which would accommodate over a hundred people. This was something new, being father-in-law to a man who did things so differently from anyone else. Then, he would end—everyone be sure and come!

Back in Olives, Lu-seng was in a quandary. Whom should he ask to be his best man? This or that one might feel slighted if not asked, so finally he decided he would have no best man at all. Word was sent to Mary of this decision, but it was added that she could do as she liked about a bridesmaid. She too was having her problem. In Lisuland it is not customary to ask one's sister to be bridesmaid, so there was no difficulty about Martha. (Second Sister had now been named Martha.) But there were Lydia, Rachel and others. One must be careful not to offend, because this was not just Mary's wedding. Oh no. This was *Lu-seng's wedding*! So when the message was brought that Lu-seng had decided to go unattended, that relieved Mary. She would go unattended too.

It was really going to be an important affair. Ma-pa was coming over from Oak Flat for the ceremony, and bringing a distinguished Chinese guest with him—Dr. Wesley May, who had been trained in America and spoke English; he wanted to take their picture.

November 13th dawned a beautiful day. Golden autumn lay upon the mountains. The rice had been harvested and the buckwheat was reddening in the fields. Blue skies overhead, snowy peaks to put a tang in the air, pine trees to lend their perfumed needles for a carpet for the chapel, and the wine-plush flowers of buckwheat glowing out from between the cornfields, where the stubble lay a pale gold in the sunshine. It was good to be alive.

Up in the centre of the village Lu-seng and his hundred guests were sending merry sounds down the village slopes as they fixed the bridal arch in place. In her father's hut at the bottom of the village Mary waited nervously. It is Lisu custom for the bridegroom and his friends to come for the bride ringing a gong as they travel over the high trails. Her family then give them a meal, after which they return to the chapel in the bride-groom's village and the ceremony takes place. Being in the same village, there would be no feast at Mary's house, and Lu-seng, unattended, would go down alone for her. Hour after hour she waited patiently whilst her girl friends fluttered in and out with bits of news. None of them guessed the rea reason for the delay. It was that Lu-seng who had so often lectured other young people as to what was the proper behaviour at a wedding, when his own hour arrived was suddenly seized with panic! He had a terrifying desire to run away! He kept making one excuse after another to delay that journey down the hill for his bride. He said that this must yet be done and that was necessary, until at length no subterfuge was left. It was inescapable. A white man, a noted Chinese physician and one hundred guests—he must go through with it. So ten o'clock in the morning saw Lu-seng, his mouth firmly set, descend the hill to Father Jiu's shanty. Gathered near the doorway was a group of heathen who nudged one another, tittered and whispered. Looking grim, the young bridegeroom entered the house, turned to the little bride sitting there timidly and said, "Let's go!" Whereupon they started on the climb to the chapel, the man first, according to Oriental etiquette.

Thus it fell out, as so often in human life, that he who had lectured others on how to be married was nervous and fidgety, whilst she who had feared that her inexperience might lead to a *faux pas* sat trim and correct, answered in a sweet, clear voice easily heard, and was the most perfect bride the district had seen!

But all things, even the embarrassment of being married in church, come to an end. Lu-seng, who afterwards told Ma-ma of this inward conflict added, "But as soon as the ceremony was over the joy returned! The rest of the day was gloriously happy —it was only for that little while."

And thus two stones of fire were set together.

There is a common and fallacious idea abroad in young Western minds that God chooses two such lives for the one and only purpose of human happiness. It would be wiser to acknowledge the truth that God, although He delights to give happiness, has also something much higher in view. The analogy might make it clearer.

The opal is usually cut with a smooth surface called *en cabochon*, but the fire-opal is frequently faceted. This brings out greater beauty in light and colour. To facet, each stone is set in a cuplike instrument called a "dop", and then they are rubbed against each other until the facet is produced. This is the work of a lapidary and requires great care and skill. For instance, the famous Cullinan diamond took nine months to cut. God often does a similar work with His stones of fire, if He sees that they warrant facets. And as the trials and pressure of two lives adjusting to one another, together with circumstances from without, are brought to bear on these two, do not forget the Master lapidary as He bends with skill and love and care over them.

5

War—as Diamond Dust

DIAMOND dust mixed with oil is the only material used in polishing precious stones. It is put upon fast rotating wheels called "skaifs" (2,500 revolutions per minute) and the gem is held against them. In other words, a quick succession of hard, unconquerable particles pressed against the jewel will polish it. The spiritual counterparts, as God brings them into human lives, especially at certain periods, are sharp painful events that follow fast one upon another, all of them irresistible, cannot be pushed away, must be accepted and endured. When the skaif is removed, one sees the beautiful lights of patience, self-sacrifice and humility shining forth. Mortals call it war. Those who watch it from above, see it as the Master lapidary's diamond dust polishing His stones of fire.

And now the greatest happiness of human life had come to Mary—a husband she adored, a comfortable private home and an ideal to work for together. The service of the Lord was a passion in both their young hearts. And the first thing on the horizon was the Christmas festival.

This was the first year that Village of the Olives were hosts to the church at Christmas, and it entailed a lot of work. Last Christmas there had been one thousand Lisu to the festival; this time the guerilla soldiers in the canyon would cause many to hesitate about leaving their homes, but at least hundreds would come. Much firewood must be cut and certain jobs of cooking, cutting meat, serving tables and so on, apportioned. In previous festivals the eating arrangements had not been well organized, Lu-seng thought, and he had other ideas how to make everything go faster, taste better and occupy less time. Nightly the little chapel meetings overflowed with youthful vim and interest. They had asked Ma-ma to translate a new Christmas song which only they would know, and now they must practise it in four parts so as to be able to surprise the guests.

Also there were two more weddings to be performed—Enoch to Sarah and Tychicus to Chloe. Pastor Luke had brought his family over for a vacation (although he himself taught them each night) and married the two couples. The village buckwheat also was still being harvested, and as each family helps the other, Mary would be called on now and again for exchange labour, as previously promised. Also Lu-seng left his New Year's suit of clothes for his little bride to sew, and clever Elizabeth (Luke's wife) helped her with the difficult parts. That was Lu-seng's favourite suit; long after it was in holes he insisted it be patched again and again that he might continue to wear it.

Then there was Lu-seng's household, with whom Mary must now live and work. Lu-seng-pa, with his funny puns, was a gentle, kindly man that everyone liked. Lu-seng-ma ruled the home—except when her son was present. His ability to talk, organize and think quickly was undoubtedly inherited from his mother. It was her clever planning and bargaining which really supported the family. Older than all of them (she was sixty when Lu-seng married) she ran around and superintended everything like a young girl. Mary must now learn Lu-seng-ma's way of feeding the pigs and chickens, cooking a hot mash for the cow when it calved, making bean and pepper pickle (Lu-seng-ma's skill was famous; others came to buy her pickle) and a hundred and one other things.

Also there were Timothy and little John, Homay's son. Timothy, Lu-seng's cousin, herded the cows and helped with the ploughing. Big-hearted Lu-seng-ma had offered to take in little John, but now that he was walking he was beginning to be a problem. His father was so often away on long preaching trips, and not being her own child, the kind woman was slow to discipline him, with inevitable results. Mary had to share in unpleasant situations which arose, but for her first few years among them these burdens did not weigh heavily.

That Christmas festival was pronounced the best ever held. The new arrangements for eating and cooking had worked well. To Mary had fallen the job of being one of the cooks, for that was easily the hardest and least popular. The stoves, merely holes cut in a bank of earth, supported a big iron cauldron of water, into which the steamer of corn was placed, the fire burning underneath. It took hours to get done and the cooks must rise at four in the morning, standing in the bleak wind to watch that it did not burn. It was hard to get volunteers for such a task, so Mary accepted it, and she was the only one who never had to be personally called for that early rising hour. Her quiet loyalty to Lu-seng and his ideals was one of the beautiful colours in this little opal.

Just one thing happened to cast a shadow of warning about the year to come. Chinese soldiers arrived from Place of Action on the last evening of the festival, came to the platform and reminded the church that there was a war being fought, and that they should be loyal to China. (Some of the heathen tribes at the border had welcomed the Japanese.) But no one dreamed it was so close to them. A vote of thanks had been given to the village of the Olives and a suggestion that everyone would like to come again next year. But as it turned out, five years passed before Ma-ma was able to celebrate Christmas with them again.

To Mary the word "Japan" was unpronounceable and of the vaguest import. Her thoughts quickly left the ominous warning to prepare with deepest pleasure for the February Girls' Bible School.

The three brides from Olives all were going—Mary, Sarah and Chloe: their husbands would escort them and carry their loads. Brother Three was away on a trip and Lu-seng had been asked to teach on the staff until Brother Three got back. Great were the expectations and plans, but when the day of departure came it was stormy, a snow blizzard on the mountains. To walk a day's journey in the rain in cold February might lead to sickness, for Lisu have no umbrellas or raincoats and would get soaked through. There was no help for it, they must wait until the weather cleared. How anxiously they prayed on Sunday but still the skies were leaden. Lu-seng had gone on ahead to help Ma-ma with the housing and dormitory problems and Mary thought about him all day—how disappointed he would be that they had not arrived. Both were looking forward to this their first school together—Lu-seng was planning to help her make up her sermon outlines when it came her turn to address the big Sunday noon service at Oak Flat. Would she be able to go now? Already the first Sunday of the school was passing—this weather could keep up for two weeks; it often did in February.

It was still grey and dark-looking, all the grand jagged mountain peaks were out of sight, covered by a blanket of low hanging clouds, and even the lower slopes had that dull, drenched appearance which is so depressing; but the little band started out.

How pretty Mary looked as she came in that afternoon. Her cheeks were rosy from the exertion and happy anticipations, and her pearly teeth glimpsed in her shy smiles. Lu-seng met them in the church kitchen, and after shaking hands a spell seemed to have fallen upon him, so that he could not tear himself from Mary's vicinity. One excuse or another provided him with jobs near where she was, so that he could see her.

There was a new member of the staff this year, Eva Tseng. Eva was a Chinese pastor's daughter who had come to help Mama in the house in exchange for lessons in Bible, music and English. She was to be on the staff of this G.B.S., teaching them knitting, an art entirely unknown in that part of the canyon at that time. The first evening, after service, the young husbands sat around the fire in the girls' dormitory shanty and chatted for a while. Eva, wishing to get acquainted with everyone, joined them. When drum taps sounded, they all dispersed and Ma-ma asked Eva what they had been doing.

"Oh just talking—all but Lu-seng. He was writing. He wrote 'Mary, Mary, Mary' in English—a whole page of nothing else! What would he want to do that for?" Eva was mystified, but not Ma-ma. Love has to have an outlet, and little Mary, who by this time knew her name in English, must have been thrilled to see that page and to understand the silent tongue which felt no freedom in public. It was her welcome to school.

Obstetrics and Mothercraft were taught for the first time that February. The influence of these schools was undoubtedly great. The Lisu are animists and are taught from birth that sickness is only caused by the bite of a demon. If you propitiate the demon by a blood sacrifice, then you will get better. To teach them that disease comes from germs which breed best in dirt and darkness means a mental revolution of all their thinking and attitude toward life. There is still much to be accomplished, but personal cleanliness at least has greatly increased, especially in some districts like Olives, as a mere comparison of photographs, new and old, shows. And the mixing with other girls from both sides of the canyon has had a broadening effect upon all.

After Closing Day Mary had to hurry home, for a new venture was about to be started. A two weeks' school for teenage boys, the cowherd class, was to be tried, and Timothy wanted to attend, so Mary must watch the cows until he got back.

That school for boys was not without excitement—indeed, the staff wondered if there could be a school at all! Those days the heavy drum-m-m of airplanes overhead intensified the rumours that the enemy was now only two days' journey away; the postmaster had fled into hiding and the Post Office was empty. Would boys be allowed away from home under such conditions? Friends and families were saying that if the Japanese got any nearer the ferry boat would be destroyed, and then return home for those on the west bank would be rendered impossible. Everyone knew that Chinese soldiers were already at the crossing awaiting the order to wreck the ferry. So assembling day was one of interest and ended in praise —thirty-six boys arrived! Full to overflowing, for the last two had to sleep on Ma-ma's premises—the two little shanty dormitories had no room for them.

What blessed days followed. Outside Lisuland was at its loveliest—snow-capped peaks still dazzling white from new-fallen snow, but golden sunshine pouring down into moist brown earth and the peach trees putting forth their delicate pink, a spiritual metaphor of new life. And into those thirty-six young hearts, moistened (so to speak) by opportunity and with danger, the Word of God was pouring, and even though it was only for two weeks, at the end these human buds seemed to have put forth tokens of resurrection life at work within. A little growth was noticeable in this one and that one.

They were allowed a Closing Day programme too and Timothy won the honour of being elected as conductor of music for the occasion! His marks were high also, so, as he sped home over the long, winding trails, he felt a new exhilaration and desire to progress which he had never experienced before. Always he had sat in the shadow of Lu-seng's knowledge and ability, which was discouraging to one so slow. But that same cousin's careful tutoring had produced something not recognizable until Timothy got away from Lu-seng's brilliance and among boys of just his own age. Now he felt that there was the power of accomplishment within him, and when he reached home his tongue flew so fast that (Lu-seng told Ma-ma) no one else could get a word in edgewise! We can imagine that happy fireside: those three Bible students comparing experiences while the ruddy flames threw rosy lights upon their joy.

Timothy's experience was an indirect enrichment of Mary's life. More and more now the ploughing and planting fell upon these two, and as they worked together they would review Bible verses or Christian songs.

* * *

The year 1943, which had begun so sunnily, was doomed to end in trial unthinkable and never before experienced.

During the spring and summer the Chinese guerilla forces had pushed into Burma, but by the end of September the Japanese had compelled them to retreat into China. The Japanese, having won the friendship of the heathen tribes around the Burma Road, had gained the lower reaches of the Salween in consequence, and were reported advancing up the canyon.

It was toward the end of October that word spread one afternoon that soldiers were approaching the Village of the Olives itself. Soldiers of which side could not be known until they drew closer, but in any case it was bad news for the Lisu. Silently and anxiously, those out in the fields or watching the cattle on the hills returned to their huts. As the long file drew within recognition distance, the word was shouted by the town crier, "Chinese soldiers will bivouac here. Ju-kwey-tsai and Bo-tsai-yi will cut grass for the colonel's mules to eat!" and so on. Demur was not only hopeless but would breed trouble; silent glances from one to the other were eloquent and a small source of comfort. Gradually the word leaked out that the Japanese had arrived at the other side of the mountain (which is Burma) and another group were only two days' south in the canyon. This regiment of guerillas would camp in Olives, and since there were no other dwellings, take over the homes of the Lisu.

Up the trail to Lu-seng's fields rode the colonel. He dismounted at the sight of their new house, walked in, looked around, approved its cleanliness and space, and stated, "This will be my headquarters." Scared and shy, little Mary slipped in and tried to gather up her bedding, books, clothing—whatever she dared—with bold Chinese soldiers looking on. Where should she take them? The colonel's aide-de-camp had taken over Thomas' shanty, so all she could do was carry her things into Lu-seng-ma's hut and stack them on top of the grain cupboard in the small granary which led off the one main room. Two soldier servants were already in that one room, overhauling Lu-seng-ma's pots to see which to use for cooking the colonel's supper. They brought practically no equipment, so just "borrowed" the Lisu's. There are no stores in the canyon from which they could be replenished, for the iron pots are carried by the Lisu from a Chinese town four days' journey away to the south; with the Japanese already on that road, there would be no possibility of purchase or travel even in the near future. Mary just had to stand helplessly by and wait until the soldiers leisurely cooked and ate a meal, and then her pots, unwashed, would be free for her to use. This was happening in every other shanty in the village. These soldiers were all heathen, which meant dishonest. Their one brass tea-kettle disappeared when these men finally left, but that is getting ahead of our story.

The colonel said he was sorry, but this was war. He did add that he intended to see that his men behaved themselves and that if there was any stealing or dissatisfaction the Lisu should report to him and he would punish the offender.

That night as the little Christian group met in their chapel, Chinese soldiers stalked curiously in and sat down to look and listen. Most of them did not understand the Lisu language, so the young people were free to whisper and compare their trials.

"You've lost your house, Mary, haven't you? Are you going to move up to the caves or live with Lu-seng-ma? There are three soldiers in our small shanty and I will have to sleep on the floor."

"Two practically live in Lu-seng-ma's house, though," said Mary. "They cook for the colonel and we cannot eat until they have finished—they use our fire and our pots. Lu-seng-ma, Lu-seng-pa, Timothy, little John and I, all have to live there."

"You've got the granary and the porch, when it is not too cold."

"Yes; we're making do. It might be worse."

"Will Lu-seng go to Bible School and leave you in conditions like that?"

"If he wants to. I promised I would never hinder him," and her young jaw set firmly even while she lowered her head quickly to hide the tears. She never broke that promise. "Passion held by principle."

That year of 1943 the R.S.B.S. had been split into three separate months of study, April, August and November. The reason was the birth of Ma-ma's little son, Daniel, in August; and the date for gathering for the November school was only four days away.

That night, after the soldiers had finally departed and the door was barred, Lu-seng-ma brought the question up.

"You can't leave us now and go to Bible school," she said to her son in her decisive, energetic way.

"I'm praying about it," he answered evasively. "These soldiers aren't likely to offend Mary with the colonel so close. He knows that Ma-pa loves us very much, and an offence to us would be sure to reach Ma-pa's ears. I'm more worried about the rest of the Christians—and the chapel. It is empty during the day and I saw soldiers eyeing it to-night."

"Well, we are in such danger and such inconvenience I do not think you should go," stoutly declared Lu-seng-ma, who adored her son and always tried to keep him near.

"You're not in danger with one hundred soldiers to protect you. And one less person in this small room would be one less inconvenience," replied her invincible son.

"You go across the river and you might never get back!" wailed the disappointed mother.

And so silent little Mary knew that her dearly beloved had decided to go.

The next day Lu-seng's fear for the chapel materialized. He found some soldiers pushing the benches together and spreading out their bedding. Then it was he made up his mind. To approach that Chinese colonel was not an easy thing. No soldier dared approach him carelessly; they must bow at each step they took toward his august presence. But the colonel was living in Lu-seng's house, so, with much inward prayer, like Nehemiah of old, this barefoot Lisu lad asked for an interview with the great man.

"Well, Lu-seng, what do you want?"

"Sir, you said we might report if your men did anything untoward. Some are moving into our chapel. I am sorry, but we cannot let them have that. They are in our homes and using our things and we have said nothing, for we realize that this is war. But our chapel is different. It is holy, the place where we worship God and the only place where we can gather for that purpose. We use it every night."

"I will see about it." The colonel's words were curt and Lu-seng's face as he left the house was grim and set. As Mary went to draw water at the water-hole, she whispered the news to the other girls there, and soon most of the Christians in the village knew that their chapel was in peril, knew too of Lu-seng's brave request, and much heart prayer poured up to the Father all day. There was absolutely no place in their homes now to pray or read, and there were such constant trials. A spoon was missing from this house, a chicken had disappeared from that—things too small to report to the colonel, but someone must obviously stay in each hut all the time to watch what was done. For instance, while Teacher Thomas was away that next month, the soldiers occupying his hut took out his Bible notes of the years and tore out the pages, some from each notebook, to roll their tobacco into home-made cigarettes. Such a loss was irreparable, as those notes were not in mimeograph, but hand written. Daily there was loss and grief and tension. The buckwheat was not yet cut; whatever would they do when harvest time arrived and they must eat early to be out in the fields at the first break of daylight, for days were shorter now? The soldiers always would eat first. They must have the comfort of their nightly gatherings for prayer at least. "O Lord, spare our chapel!" was their inward cry.

That evening, as dusk fell, the chapel was speedily occupied. Every Christian was present, and that meant an audience mainly under thirty years of age. After the first song, the door was darkened by the tall form of the Chinese guerilla colonel, who stalked up the aisle to the platform followed by his interpreter. Lu-seng silently stepped off the platform and left it to them.

"I have said to you, Villagers of the Olives, that I would do my best to be just and fair to you," began the colonel pleasantly, his interpreter turning it quickly into Lisu. "Now we all realize that this is a time of war and things cannot be as comfortable for anyone as in normal times. My men need housing and they would like to borrow your chapel here. I am not going to force it, but I am going to ask you—all of you who are willing to *lend* us this house, which is empty during each day, for the time we are here, please put your hand up!"

There was silence while the colonel waited expectantly. Not a hand was raised. The colonel, somewhat nettled, thought his interpreter had not made it clear. "Put it this way. Everyone who is *not* willing to lend us your chapel put your hand up!"

Immediately every hand in the room was raised, the young faces scared, but set, the hands silent but determined. "Stones of fire."

The colonel was obviously chagrined, but he had trapped himself. He had said that he would not force it. He had been sure that they would consent, if only to curry his favour. With grim countenance he answered, "Well, then, the chapel is yours. I will give orders." And he stalked down the aisle and out of the door.

Oh what relief! Oh what praises to God, guarded and quiet,

for Chinese soldiers were still at the back watching. So it came to pass that through the long months of strain which followed there was always the heart consolation, "At eventide there will be peace"; peace in His presence, joy of fellowship, comfort of mutual consolations. Before long the colonel issued a second order. "The close of the Christians' chapel service is to be curfew for this village. Anyone found on the trails after the Christians have retired will be taken as a spy." His men watched all the trails into the village now, night and day, for the Japanese were only two days' journey to the south and a second group of them had reached the other side of the mountain on which Olives lies.

With conditions thus, Lu-seng and Thomas set out for the November Bible School. We can be certain that somewhere, sometime, Lu-seng had had a talk with Mary. He had assured her of his love, told her of the Bible verse God had given him assuring him that she and the family would be safe until his return. So the night of October 30th saw Lu-seng and Thomas cosily esconced in House of Grace telling Ma-ma this thrilling story.

And now little Mary was left to the difficult task of life in overcrowded quarters, the buckwheat crop to harvest and many another trial. But He who has promised that we shall not be tempted above that we are able to bear sent her a consolation. Her silent but shy, wistful look at parting had haunted her husband, and as soon as he had opportunity at Oak Flat, he typed a long, three-page letter to her and his mother, telling of his love, and if he had been wrong to insist on coming, to forgive. It was signed, "Your worthless Lu-seng." She carried that letter tucked in her blouse next her heart all the time as she went about her work. He made mistakes sometimes, her impetuous, strong-headed boy, but he wasn't worthless. Oh no.

During the day the boom of distant cannon brought an anxious look to her eyes. She had never seen a cannon. They said that this one belonged to the Japanese on the Burma Pass, which was three days' journey away. It must be a tremendous gun which could make such a big sound from such a distance. Of course, as a bird flies over the mountains it was not so far, but the Lisu never think of distance that way. Then the soldiers who cooked for the colonel told her that the Japanese in the canyon had retreated two days to the south, though the group on the Pass were still there, so she felt a little more easy.

About this time another matter brought joy and happiness. Martha had also received a like-letter and old Father Jiu, after stuttering all over the village about losing two good-looking daughters to Christian husbands who would not pay him any dowry, at last consented. Manasseh, the prospective groom, was well off as Lisu go. He and his family were among the highest tax-payers in the village, and as he had been a Christian since he was small he was a clean lad, grown strong and tall. The wedding took place that autumn, and Mary and Martha were knit together in a new bond, which only grew stronger as the years passed. Manasseh was Lu-seng's first cousin, so the relationship was pleasant. Running into Martha's new little house, which was close by Lu-seng's, was a new experience and the days passed quickly and happily until Lu-seng should return.

But the sunshine of life was doomed to have many a cloud those days. Into Village of the Olives came a new menace in the person of a Chinese man named Tsao. He announced that he had been sent by the Government to open a school and teach Chinese to the Lisu. The Chistians did not pay him much attention, because the Lisu church had opened its own school over at Oak Flat, but he was very active and went everywhere in the village urging the need of the knowledge of Chinese and trying to get students. With Chinese soldiers in their homes to whom they could not talk, the benefit of a knowledge of Chinese was felt, and Tsao's exhortations were certainly timely.

Into this situation walked Lu-seng on his return. How glad he was to get home to Mary! That morning he had arisen at dawn so as to be able to start out at the first streaks of daylight, and he had arrived by noon. One of the first things that met Lu-seng was this village talk of Tsao. He had noticed that no Christian came to study under him and he had deliberately set himself to win them. He invited them to meals with him and held up the opportunities of Government service to a Lisu who could read and write Chinese. He could get them free education in Tali city, he urged, if they would first come and learn the elements under him.

Now, ever since he had become a Christian, Lu-seng had thirsted for more education. Ma-pa and Ma-ma knew this, but they had also noticed that knowledge of Chinese was often a hindrance to a Lisu Christian. The feudal lairds immediately laid hold of such, pressed him into their own personal service, perhaps to keep their trade accounts, writing letters for law cases and so on, and that Lisu was lost to the Lord's work. Moreover, those lairds' feudal castles were hotbeds of sin; it was a rare Christian who could live in that atmosphere without harm. Ma-ma had suggested that Lu-seng learn English as an approach for further education, but he had not made good progress. He did not know the discipline of study, would not bother to try to understand the grammatical constructions (of which the Lisu language has very few) and thought he should be able to get along with just memorizing nouns and verbs. He had become discouraged over English and was just ripe for Tsao's invitation.

The only time the matter could be discussed was late at night after the soldiers had had their leisurely smoke and retired. So it was on one of those nights that Lu-seng, poking the hot ashes out from under the blazing flames and popping corn in them, started on the subject that was closest to his heart. Lu-seng-ma and Lu-seng-pa were in bed, little John slept on the floor under Lu-seng-pa, and possibly Mary had retired to the top of the big wooden granary in the end room.

"I've about made up my mind to stop preaching for a while and study Chinese," began Lu-seng casually. Mary, from her dark corner, pulled the blanket off her face and listened.

"I cannot get anywhere until I know something more than Lisu. English has the most educational books, but I see now I am not getting enough to be able to read them. If I had more Chinese," (he spoke a bit of trade Chinese already), "I would have the whole Bible. I can only have the Lisu New Testament now. Who knows when the missionaries will get the rest translated? And if I knew Chinese, I would not be afraid to go to more distant places to preach. As it is now, with this war on, and soldiers on the roads cross-questioning you every few miles, I dare not go afield. I've been thinking it back and forth and I've about decided to drop everything and just concentrate on Chinese."

His mother was alert and listening now, too.

"Well, then you could do that right here in the village," she said, delighted at this prospect of keeping her beloved son close at hand. "Mr. Tsao would be glad to teach you."

"Yes," answered Lu-seng a bit impatiently, for he penetrated her secret thoughts. "But I would soon have to go off to Tali city, and that would be for five years. You have to promise to stay five years, and it would take that to really get Chinese ingrained into one, which is my desire."

Now his mother was awake for certain. She pushed herself to a sitting posture with those quick decisive movements so characteristic of her.

"Five years! O my son. I'd be dead before you got back. Remember, I'm an old woman—I'm sixty-two this year!"

A smile flickered over her son's face as with his chopsticks he dexterously flipped a popped corn into his hand and then into his mouth.

"But you're quite strong yet, Mother. It is only ten days' journey away. If you were really ill, I'd come home—they'd give me leave of absence for that."

The old lady moaned. "But you're married! You wouldn't take Mary with you?"

The silent little listener on top of the granary cupboard was also sitting upright now.

"No, of course not. There aren't any women in that school. Besides, you need her help and she would get homesick for Lisuland. We would have to separate for five years. She is only nineteen now. We are both young. We belong to one another —that is settled. We have no children. This is the time to do it. In five years' time she will be twenty-four and I will be twenty-nine—just right if we are going to have a family. As I see it I must go now or never."

In the dark little granary Mary put her hand to her heart to hold quiet its loud beating. "We've no children." Was it really true—*now*? Lu-seng did not know yet. She wasn't sure herself. She could not be absolutely sure for several weeks yet. Oh what would she do? Not see Lu-seng for five years? No sun in her sky for five long years? Oh how could she live. She lay back quietly and prayed, "Lord, I promised I would not hinder his study. Oh help me! Five years. O Lord, how could I live? But it is true—Oh I thank Thee—it is true that he belongs to me and I to him; nothing can change that. Should I tell him about . . .? Maybe it would change his mind. Oh I dare not. If I were wrong, he would blame me always. I'd be the one who hindered his education and—I *promised*, O Lord, help me to *endure*." "Passion held by principle." Long years afterward Lu-seng spoke of his wife one night in these quiet words: "She had wonderful powers of endurance." But they were won by prayer, the gift of the Spirit of God. How the Lord must love His little opals; hearts of fire held fast by clear, translucent stone. Deep in His pocket where no one can see. How His fingers must close around them and love each touch of them. And they too, when they quieten themselves, can feel His Hand. "The beloved of the Lord shall dwell in safety by him: and the Lord shall cover him all the day long." Mary was to learn through the tempestuous days ahead the quietening peace of the touch of His Hand.

Christmas was now rapidly approaching. To hold it in Olives with soldiers overflowing the place was impossible, even if permission could have been obtained for such large numbers to cross the river. So it was voted to have two celebrations. But a quotation from the letters of the time will make it clearer.

"*December 29th, 1943.* It was the week before Christmas, a bright, sunny morning with hope and expectation in the air. Suddenly Eva came running in, 'Ma-ma, go look!' she cried, 'Luchang is burning. Japanese maybe?' I rushed outside and from the brow of a mountain on the opposite bank of the canyon to us a column of smoke was rising high; soon it was followed by a second column, then a third and then flames were visible. The town of Luchang is our county seat and the

Japanese had been in its vicinity for nearly two months. Then as we watched, the roar of cannon belched forth and the fight was on.

"Previously the fighting had been low down, on the banks of the river probably, so the sound of it had reached us as muffled and far-away. But Luchang is on an altitude level with us, only a few miles away as the crow flies, and the firing sounded very close. The great rocky crags above us caught up the cannon roar and grumbled it angrily to one another until that belch of death seemed a continuous sound swirling around our heads. It was rather awful.

"We wasted a morning packing for flight! Then, as the next morning greeted us with still more vivid flames from a third burning village, we wasted (!) a second hour or so discussing where to flee; then as everything has continued quiet ever since, and our side say the others have retreated, we wasted a third hour unpacking to stay! Such is life in the midst of war.

"But that was the start of Christmas. As the river has been uncrossable except by military order, we had decided on two celebrations, one on this side at our village, and one on that side at Sandalwood Flat. Unfortunately, both places are uncomfortably near to Luchang, so we wondered how many would dare to come. Brother Three has not felt strong since his rheumatic fever, so it was decided that Ma-pa take the festival on that side and Brother Three the one on this side."

Luchang is only a long day's journey from Olives. Some thirty-three miles? And news of its burning and the shooting was soon brought to Mary by the colonel's spies. But the Chinese seemed to have been victorious, so Mary planned to go along with Lu-seng and other young people to Christmas at Sandalwood Flat.

They had a good time with the 120 others who met for that celebration. Lu-seng, of course, was watching for an opportunity to have a talk with Ma-pa over his new plans, and he found one time when Ma-pa was alone for a few minutes. Ma-pa was immediately alarmed as he listened to the eager young ambitions, but was too wise to show it. "Tsao is a heathen," he said slowly. "I hate to see you have to study under such—and you would soon find their godless atmosphere intolerable. Why not come over to Oak Flat and study under the Mr. Yang in the church school? You would have to sit with the six-year-olds to begin with, but with your mind you would soon be far beyond them, and it would be good to start right from the beginning and get a proper foundation. Then when you have gone through all their readers you are ready for higher education. We of the China Inland Mission have a hospital at Tali—you could take your five years of Chinese under us. I think that would be better."

Lu-seng was delighted. He had expected Ma-pa to object! Dreams of becoming a fluent Chinese scholar, of travel, of new knowledge, new experiences, thrilled him. He was gay and voluble all the way home as the little band from Olives went down the steep hillside together. Mary watched him anxiously. She was beginning to know her beloved. She had seen him talking with Ma-pa; then Ma-pa must have consented, or Lu-seng would not be so happy. Well, she would know to-night. And so she did.

It was hardest for Lu-seng-ma. She knew she could never change her son once he had made up his mind, but she had hoped that he would be home for a year, studying under Tsao right here in her own village. Now he had said he must pack up immediately and go right over to Oak Flat. Lu-seng-ma groaned and sighed, but no one paid any attention to her. Mary was busy getting ready to go to Girls Bible School in February. At least she and Lu-seng would have that month together in Oak Flat, he in the Chinese school and she in the Bible school, and he had promised to help her with her sermon outlines again for week-end preaching.

War news was not very good. The Japanese had returned to Luchang! But the Chinese guerilla soldiers were still in the village of Olives and Mary would soon be coming over for G.B.S., so Lu-seng started out for his new experience as a student of Chinese with an eager happy heart.

February 5th was the date set for the Girls' School to assemble, and Ma-pa sent word by soldier reporters that he and Lu-seng would meet them at the river bank and see them across, for no one might cross without military permit now. Ma-pa had obtained that for all of them. It was a merry party that set out. Sarah and Chloe each had babies so could not come; but Martha was coming for her first time, and Mary, Lydia and Rachel for their third time. Rhoda also came, and Anna, Miriam and Susanna—Olives girls in all were eight. Then they must wait at the river bank for Sandalwood Flat girls and those from Little Olives. It was fun on the rocky shore waiting for all to gather. They could see Lu-seng and Ma-pa on the eastern bank and they hallooed back and forth. When they saw the ferry start out, they saw Lu-seng get in. "Is he going to row?" asked one. Yes, Lu-seng knew how to row and the boatmen were glad of his help, for the current was strong and it took all their might to swing the ferry out of it. Now the swift current of mid-river had caught the frail craft and was whirling it downstream. How the boatmen yelled and bent their strong backs to guide it over and through the swirling waters. The girls who had never crossed before were scared, but Mary and the others comforted them. It is true that more than once the ferry had capsized and drowned most of those on board, but not usually at this season of the year. Soon the boat was approaching their rocks, a man in the prow with a hook on a long stick was holding it out to catch hold of a jutting rock, and then with a shout they were anchored.

Lu-seng was the first one out. He leaped from the boatside before it beached and landed on the soft sand. Then came the handshaking and Lu-seng's exhortations to the new girls. "Wait until everyone is out of the boat before you try to jump in; then, when you do, be careful not to step on their oars or that will bring them bad luck!"

Such a happy band and such a waggle of tongues. Everyone wanted to see Ma-ma's baby son. They heard he had red hair and just could not imagine what red hair was like on a human being! Lu-seng, who thought it pretty, had been allowed to give the baby a bath.

"Bath him—you mean spit water over him like we do?"

"Oh no," says Lu-seng. "He goes right into a zinc tub, under the water—all but his face. It is warm water. Ma-ma has it heated."

"Oh how cruel!" cried one of the girls. "The poor little fellow."

"Not at all," grinned Lu-seng. "He is not a bit scared. In fact, he loves it; kicks and splashes and cries when he has to come out!"

Then the tongues did wag, "He got a bath like that every day? And he did not catch cold nor get sick? Well the marvels of these white people will never be all told." No one noticed how steep the climb across the river was, that day. The white baby was a sufficient theme to take them all the way to Oak Flat.

Ma-ma took advantage of this new interest to continue lessons in mothercraft. The girls were brought in, three or four at a time, each morning to observe baby Danny have a bath, be dressed, and put to sleep by himself in a native basket under the shade of the gnarled old oak trees. No baby in that part of the canyon ever slept by himself, so it caused much wonder and comment. The value of proper feeding, sleeping hours, fresh air and cleanliness were pointed out, every single one of those items being an entirely new idea to them.

During these talks together Ma-ma definitely aimed at what St. Paul termed "the transforming of your minds" and the casting out of heathen thoughts and attitudes often unconsciously retained. The announcement of the birth of a little one invariably brought titters from some girls and looks of shame from others. Both were definitely not Scriptural. Children are the gift of God and girl friends should not avoid a young mother as if she had done something wrong (which is heathen custom) but give her joy that God has entrusted her with a little life to be trained for Him.

To this end Ma-ma had composed words to the tune of "Sweet and low" based on "Where did you come from, baby dear?" turning the thoughts on the unspoiled purity of the little ones as they come to us fresh from God. This met with instant acceptance from Mary, whose secret Ma-ma did not yet know, but she could hardly have helped her more if she had known.

Putting the precious life on such a high plane, making it an ideal toward which one should reverently strive, was a deep and blessed joy.

But Mary received still another spiritual gift from this particular school. First Peter the third chapter was being taught, and when it came to "holy women of old", Ma-ma had each girl take a different Bible character for Closing Day presentation. They must give at least one spiritual lesson from each "holy woman's" life, and to Mary fell the study of Mary of Bethany. The Bible Mary's quiet insistence that spiritual things come first in this life of ours was a new angle, also the importance of times alone with God just worshipping. She knew that Lu-seng made this a rule, but the value of it had not fully come home to her before. Martha had insisted that physical things— a good meal for instance—were of equal importance, but Christ Himself had definitely sided with Mary, saying, "But one thing is needful and Mary hath chosen the better part." From this year forward this Lisu Mary chose the better part, and six years later the difference in her life and influence compared with other classmates, who did not persevere but soon slipped back into Martha-ways, was very marked. "Let her alone; she hath wrought a good work," said the Lord, and it never fails to be so even to-day.

*   *   *

The return journey was not sunny as the coming to school had been. A cloud had fallen upon Mary which had taken the smile from her face. Lu-seng had had a difference with his beloved missionaries, had thrown up study under Mr. Yang, and gone back to Olives to study, where he could do as he liked. Mary was ashamed and worried. She knew Lu-seng's impetuosity, but also his deep repentance afterwards when he came to himself. It would be good to have him home, but— she wished it had been under different circumstances. She did not know what the discussion had been about, and she knew that in the crowded little shanty at home, with Chinese soldiers about who now understood some Lisu, it would not be wise to discuss it or ask questions. Once more her part must be patient waiting until it was all revealed to her. Perhaps now Lu-seng would give up the idea of going so far away from home? And her secret she could not keep for ever. Would Lu-seng be glad? Or annoyed? And so she slipped back into her place in the life of that little farm home, inconspicuous, faithful, anxious to please, but alert for every sign that might tell her what was going on within her loved one's hot heart.

Lu-seng had gone over to Tsao, spending much time with him. At home he was short-tempered and his face dark; her loved one was not happy within; that Mary was sure of from the very first day. But he talked volubly about signing up to go to Tali for five years' training under the Government. He persuaded several others from Olives to sign up too; Jason, Manasseh, Gideon and others said that if Lu-seng went they would go too. They also were studying every day under Tsao.

Recently an honour had come to Lu-seng. In the village elections for head man almost all the villagers, heathen as well as Christian, placed their hands on his head as token that he was the one they preferred! Lu-seng only twenty-five. Mary did not remember any other villager so young nominated for that position. He refused it, but carried his head a little higher now, and in her heart Mary was anxious for him. He was not spending the time with the Lord as he did. Quietly and anxiously no doubt, she tried to help him by placing his New Testament near at hand, and in other ways made it easy for him to keep up that habit of early fellowship, which, if life was to be kept from taking a wrong side-path, was of first importance. Her own quiet time had to be at night after she went to bed. But morning, noon and night her heart was sending up prayer-cries for her dear one.

Two days after returning home she heard astonishing news —there were American soldiers at the laird's *yamen*! The American army, long anxious to push into that front line of battle were deterred. Now, however, Ma-pa having suggested to the colonel that a medical unit be brought in, as the Chinese soldiers were suffering—even dying—from the dread malaria of the Salween canyon, the colonel had consented, and they were here!

A week later when Mary was returning from a long day in

the cotton fields, she heard a voice calling across their courtyard.
"Is Ma-pa here?" she asked, astounded.

Lu-seng emerging from the porch where the chicken nests
were kept, his hands full of eggs, replied, "No. American
soldiers are here. They came over from Place of Action this
morning and are to be stationed in Olives. Sounds just like
Ma-pa's voice, doesn't it?" with a light on his face that she had
not seen for days. "I pity them so with only Chinese food to
eat—white men can't take an all-native diet quickly. I know.
Mother, take them a chicken and these eggs? They will be
needed for breakfast. The Chinese soldiers do not eat until
sun-high and white men need something before that."

"But they have someone to feed them, don't they?" remonstrated his mother, for chickens and eggs were scarce com-
modities those days. The Chinese took what they liked and paid
what price they liked too.

"I heard one of them say he was hungry. He did not realize
that I understood so much English." Lu-seng's face lit up again.
"They remind me so much of Ma-pa. Their big boots go clank-
clank just like Ma-pa's always do."

Again his little wife stole a quick sharp glance at him. He
loved Ma-pa and she was quite sure that inwardly he was
grieving for the heart-separation his impetuous leaving had
brought. She sent up a little prayer that it might not last, and it
was answered more quickly than she dreamed.

As in the previous year a Boys' Bible School had been planned
to come after the Girls', and Thomas was to be one of the
teaching staff. However, when he went to apply for a river
pass (Ma-pa was again away on conference work), Tsao not
only refused to write it, but refused river passes to the eleven
west-bank boys who had planned to go. Assembling Day came
and went, yet Thomas, knowing that Ma-ma was short-staffed
this year, was still unable to proceed. Very troubled in spirit,
he came to Lu-seng to pray about the matter.

The morning of the third day of waiting, Mary saw Lu-seng
in a corner writing a letter. She had heard that a messenger was
going to the east bank and guessed the note was for Ma-ma.
It would have brought her joy if she had known that it was a

letter of contrition, asking forgiveness for his hasty departure and saying that he had just been through the most unhappy days he could remember. Living and studying with the heathen, their filthy conversation had become unbearable. Moreover, he saw that he had been a snare to others, for Tsao was now making bold to invite the Christian girls of Olives to eat with him, and was very unpleasant if they refused. Altogether it had been a most miserable time. But the coming of the American soldiers had brought things to a climax in Lu-seng's heart. "Every time they called to one another," he wrote to Ma-ma, "I could hear Ma-pa's voice; and the sound of their leather shoes would make me think Ma-pa was coming. Then I would awaken to the fact it was not he, and such a flood of love-longing for him would sweep over me." He also explained the reason for Thomas' non-appearance.

On the other bank of the Salween Ma-ma had been going through trial. Neither Ma-pa nor Brother Three were present to help her, and she had only consented to hold this school if Thomas would promise to teach some courses. Thirty-one boys had arrived and no Thomas. She had suspected the reason, but Lu-seng's letter made it definite. It did not take her long to contact this American unit (they were always dropping in for tea or a meal, anyway) and by return messenger a written river pass for Thomas and all he cared to bring with him arrived in Olives. And the next evening not only Thomas and three pupils arrived in Oak Flat, but Lu-seng also! His face was bright and joyful once more as he recounted all the miseries of his self-effort. "I know now," he confided, "that I stepped out of the will of God in dropping the ministry, and I hope I remember the lesson." Then, with fellowship so sweetly restored, he settled back to tell her again of the pleasure of having those American soldiers in their midst. "I think that some of them are Christians and wanted to tell us," he said. "When we were singing in chapel, the tall one with the red hair came near and started to sing with us, only in English! We thought he meant by that to let us know that he was a Christian too, so we all laughed and went up and shook hands."

Later it was interesting to Ma-ma to get the American version.

The six-foot-three young captain afterwards told her: "Why, they were singing the same songs I used to sing in Sunday School back home, so I just went up and sang with them." It was enjoyed on both sides.

The Boys' Bible School ended most cheerfully, for not only was there Lu-seng and Thomas to help teach, but Brother Three returned unexpectedly and threw himself wholeheartedly into lifting the responsibilities.

After Closing Day Lu-seng returned home again to Mary, his face happy for the burden on his conscience was gone. Ah, but forgiveness granted does not mean that there is no penalty to pay! Tsao, hearing now that Lu-seng had changed his mind, was furious. "You cannot recede! I have your promise which you *made to the Government*, and that of five others also. This has become a Government affair and I will take you to law." He began calling out to Mary when he met her on the path to the water-hole or elsewhere, "You get that husband of yours to change his mind or it will be the worse for him!" and the scared little maiden hung her head and hurried home with the message. But Lu-seng is not easily driven. The more Tsao pushed the more obstinate Lu-seng became. Then the whole church came in for persecution.

Ma-pa was still away and Tsao had practically a free hand. He refused passes to cross the river to any Christian. He threatened Lu-seng day and night. He accused Jonah of self-seeking while in Government service because he had ridden a horse while on an errand for the official, and Jonah was cast into prison with charges that might have taken his life. Treason was an easy accusation in those days of war. How the little group in chapel prayed each night! Lu-seng was to be the next, Tsao said, and although Lu-seng himself was dubious how far a mere school-teacher might go, Mary was terrified. She had by now to make known her precious secret to her husband, and it was a drop of sweetness in her cup of anxiety that he was delighted.

A few days later Jonah was taken out and beaten badly. He was very brave and did not let out a sound, but it was a cruel whipping, and the girls all cried.

Toward the end of May the danger to Lu-seng himself

became so real that Mary and his mother begged him to go across the river to visit Ma-pa and stay for a while. Ma-pa was now back, and while holding a Sunday service at Place of Action he called up Lu-seng on the field telephone newly established between the Chinese guerilla colonel and his men in Olives. This was the latest marvel—that people could talk over a wire half a day's journey away; Mary and Lu-seng-ma thrilled with pride when a soldier came up the hill to summon Lu-seng to the telephone, Ma-pa calling! It was the first and only time that Lu-seng ever used a telephone, but he was able to make out Ma-pa's voice and an invitation to come across the river to Oak Flat. A pass was furnished and thus Lu-seng got away! To Mary it was an answer to prayer.

Foiled in his hopes of securing Lu-seng, Tsao now turned to Christians farther away from where Ma-pa lived. In the village of La-meh the Lisu church had opened another school, with a Chinese-speaking Christian Lisu, Titus by name, as its teacher. Tsao pounced upon this, ordered it to be disbanded, had Titus thrown into prison, then beaten and sent across the river to Ma-pa with the word that if he tried to return he would be killed.

When Titus appeared at Oak Flat with this news, Rainy Season Bible School had already begun. Ma-pa, on his return, had brought a guest speaker in the form of a Chinese seminary graduate, Miss Constance Tseh by name, an exceptionally fine Bible teacher. Ma-pa translated for her, and the evangelists have never ceased to quote her illustrations, so striking and so oriental, just the kind they enjoyed and understood to the full. Lu-seng wrote long thrilled letters home and Mary wrote back. Every now and again their letters would be detected by Tsao and a translation made! After one such (a letter written by Mary it happened to be) the Chinese soldier called in to translate said "Hmph. Nothing but a love-letter to her husband—what are you worrying about?" Poor Mary hung her head in shy confusion that her outpourings to Lu-seng should be so hauled out and read in public, but she kept on trying. When the colonel had to send letters across the river, villagers from Olives were usually chosen to do this. Mary, hearing of someone appointed to carry the next epistle, by night would slip him her little bit of folded paper, and as the whole village, heathen and Christian, loved her, the messenger would tuck it into the folds of his turban and so it got across undetected.

It was August 17th when baby was born. There was no one to help the little mother but Lu-seng-ma and those instructions from Girls' Bible School. But mother and child both came through all right, and it was a boy! A very tiny son. Lu-seng-ma was enraptured, and even old Lu-seng-pa, when allowed to return to the shanty, beamed all over his wrinkled, kindly face. But no message was sent to the young father, away over in Oak Flat in Rainy Season Bible School. Heathen customs still held influence. It was Lu-seng-ma who at last got off a message, very casually worded, to her absent son. Baby was already twelve days old when his father learned of his existence.

Lu-seng tried to act unconcerned and pretend he was not excited, but the sparkle in his eyes and the toss of his head spoke volumes to those who knew him.

"Aren't you going home?" asked Ma-ma curiously.

"Oh, it is not necessary," he replied with studied nonchalance, then: "I have asked Ma-pa to name him."

"Oh, and what is the name?"

"He suggested Paul, which seems a little too grand, I did not mean to give him such a wonderful name."

"Oh, nonsense, I think Paul is a good choice. You will be Paul-pa and Mary Paul-ma?" Ma-ma had a scrutinizing twinkle in her eye.

"No, no," Lu-seng spoke warmly. "I do not want anyone to call us such. I want us to go by our Christian names."

When the parents are known by the child's name it is called "teknonymy", and the Lisu tribe practises this. Lu-seng, however, would not have it, and he was successful. Never once did Ma-ma hear anyone try to call him so.

A few days later, very early in the morning, Lu-seng appeared at Ma-ma's door. "I've got to go home," and thrusting a letter into her hand, said, "Read that!" Ma-ma read:

"DEAR LU-SENG,—I hope you are well. All the brothers and sisters send their greetings.

"Our son was born on August 17th just as the light was coming through the chinks of the wall. God gave strength and your mother helped me.

"Baby looks like me. I'm sorry. Maybe he will look like you when he grows up.

"No trouble came until these last few days, when he has been vomiting and won't eat at all now. We do not know what is wrong with him. He is getting thinner and thinner and he was only four pounds at birth. I am not asking you to come home, but we fear baby will not live. He is so tiny. Be happy, do not worry about me, but—I wish you could see our little son before he dies. Goodbye. Dwell in peace.

"The writer is Your Dear One."

It will be seen what a master letter-writer she was! No one could ever say that she had interfered with his studies and called him home; she but pulled on his heart strings until he could not stay away! By the time Ma-pa was out of bed to write him a river pass, Lu-seng had eaten and was ready for the road. While Ma-pa was writing it, Lu-seng sought Ma-ma for medicine.

After reading Mary's letter, Ma-ma made a guess at the complaint, showed him how to make a soap-stick, gave him an eye-dropper to use if the other failed, supplied a few simple baby medicines and sent him off.

We may try to picture his arrival. How fast his heart beat as he sped up the long, familiar trail and sighted the village where his dear ones were! How shy and embarrassed he would be as he entered the shanty, but if by good luck no strangers were present, how quickly he would have that small form in his own hands and arms! Inquiry showed baby was indeed very sick, but Ma-ma had guessed aright. Patiently Lu-seng tried the soap-stick. It did not succeed. Then they heated warm water and the eye dropper was used. Relief was immediate and by evening baby was sucking again and the next day was quite normal. What rejoicing! Lu-seng-ma never ceased to boast how Lu-seng had saved little Paul's life.

How minutely wee mannie was examined by that ecstatic daddy!

"His face is like Mary's, but his hands are like mine," Lu-seng wrote to Ma-ma. "I think he is a nice-looking little boy. He has no hair yet—just soft fuzz on the top of his head."

And so we must leave them temporarily.

Ma-pa, Ma-ma and Danny were now setting out on their furlough. Brother Three was staying behind with the Lisu, which was a comfort, but as the Japanese war had not ended Lisu letters would be difficult to get out of China. No censor could be expected to recognize that script.

Brother Three, of course, wrote, and when Ma-ma asked how Lu-seng and Mary were getting along he replied, "Very happy, I should say. Mary and the old mother work together in the fields, whilst Lu-seng goes around preaching. Lu-seng tore down his new house after the colonel moved out, and is rebuilding it nearer to the church. I would say that Lu-seng is the pride and glory of both Mary and the old mother. Paul is growing and could stand having his face washed a little oftener!"

And so with the murmur of human happiness, as God has planned it most sweetly for men, issuing from their little shanty on the mountainside, they must be left for a couple of years.

6

The Climax of the Lapidary's Skill

"THE most magnificent diamond in the world's history was presented to the King of England, who sent it to Amsterdam to be cut. It was put into the hands of an expert lapidary, and what do you suppose he did? He took that gem of priceless worth and cut a notch in it. Then he struck it a hard blow with his instrument, and lo! the superb jewel lay in his hand cleft in twain. . . . For days and weeks that blow had been studied and planned. Drawings and models had been made of the gem. Its quality, its defects, its lines of cleavage had all been studied with the minutest care. That blow was the climax of the lapidary's skill . . . seeming to ruin the superb precious stone, it was in fact, its perfect redemption. For from those two halves were brought two magnificent gems . . . to blaze in the crown of state."[1]

This chapter is to tell of a blow, "seeming to ruin the precious stone", but in reality its perfect redemption. Even in the world's greatest jewels there are defects and weaknesses, as they come raw from the bosom of the earth; to make them great, the Master lapidary must study and then cleave. In Mary's love for God there had long been a weak human element which must be disentangled if her worship was to be pure. She had first been attracted to God because Lu-seng loved Him! And all this time there had been adoration of Lu-seng mixed up with adoration of God. That must be corrected; if not, there was constant danger that the one might crash if the other did. So for years the great spiritual Master lapidary had been studying "the lines of cleavage", and the time was now ripe to let the blow descend.

[1] From *Streams in the Desert*.

He himself did not strike (the analogy is general, not minute); He just allowed human nature to take its course, always under His controlling hand.

Now, when war with Japan ended, it was not wise to recall women missionaries and children immediately, but some of the men responded to a call to return first. Ma-pa was among these, and so it was that the Lisu church welcomed him. After a few months of visiting them in their villages, Ma-pa announced that the Mission had asked him to take a long trip, to make a survey of the whole province—in fact, to discover how many other tribes there were as yet unreached by the gospel. He invited Lu-seng to be among those who accompanied him and of course Lu-seng was thrilled to go. The trip took seven months, but at the end of that time, Ma-ma and little Daniel were back and able to return to Lisuland with them! Some of the Girls' Bible School students made a special trip to welcome Ma-ma home. but Mary was not among these, as she could not be spared from the farm. She wrote a loving little note and hoped that in the days ahead Ma-ma and Danny could visit Olives.

After seven months away from home, it was wonderful to have Lu-seng back! The neighbours crowded in to talk with him, and the evening chapel service was very fully attended while Lu-seng gave one of his sparkling descriptions of their wonderful tour in which they had found one hundred tribes! Mary's eyes shone with pride, and Lu-seng-ma, sitting on the back bench, could not conceal her gratification, but exclaimed over and over "Marvellous! Marvellous!" nodding with joy to her neighbours. The only thing that could have seemed the least like a cloud on such a happy occasion was the attitude of Lu-seng's own son. During his long absence Lu-seng had become a stranger to little Paul and could not entice his boy even with two cakes of brown sugar. The two-year-old consistently refused to capitulate. He was master in that home. If he only howled for something Grandpa or Grandma gave it to him. In vain Mary administered gentle spankings, he soon learned he had only to cry loudly enough and the grandparents would intercede. But this person called Daddy—he looked as if he would be capable of real discipline, and little Paul quietly decided it would be wiser not to get too friendly! Patiently Lu-seng tried to coax, but his small son determinedly backed away.

Although she did not see Ma-ma immediately, Mary heard from her, for Ma-ma had brought back a new study, called the Bible Club Movement. Though really for children, young people could join too, she said. In this Club you studied the Scriptures together and also memorized verses for which you received awards occasionally to encourage you along. At the end of each year's work the Lisu award was a time at Bible School, all expenses paid. Quite a few of the young folk at Olives signed up for this memory course, but Ma-ma quietly noted that Mary was the only one of the married girls who did so. The others laughed and said they had no time. Mary was busy too, but she propped her Bible up against the weaving loom and as she wove she memorized. Timothy belonged to the club also but as he liked to do his mostly at night, they often listened to one another recite until Lu-seng-pa declared that this "babbling" every evening was getting to be a nuisance. But Mary was the first girl in all of Lisuland to complete the course. Among other things she had won a hymnbook (this particular edition was expensive for a Lisu); as for Girls' Bible School expenses, she did not need to memorize as far as that; being a teacher's wife, her board was paid by the Lisu church, nevertheless she memorized it through to the end. And later when the second year's course was offered she finished that one also.

At length the time came when Ma-ma was able to pay a visit to Olives. It was five years since she had been in their village and she saw a great change and growth. For instance, at the Welcome Arch there was added a children's choir who sang from memory in four parts, "There's a teacher at the door, let her in!" Lydia led them, and to hear small eight-year-old boys roll in their bass, "Let, Oh let her in" was amusing. Ma-ma felt rewarded for all her pains to emphasize children's work at the yearly Girls' Bible Schools. As she went down the long line shaking hands, she looked especially for her Bible girls and for Mary in particular, because she had never seen little Paul as yet. There he was tied to mother's back and pushed forward so that Ma-ma might take and shake his little hand too. Then there was Martha with Apollos on her back, and Chloe with her second son, Sarah with her second little daughter on her back, and so on. It was a joyous reunion, and Ma-ma went from home to home among those who had been her girl students, but were now kept from Bible School by the responsibilities of motherhood. Each little family seemed very happy. Rachel had married Jason and though sorrowing for the loss of their first baby, their clean little home was a shining example of what could be done with just Lisu equipment. On the door of Mary and Lu-seng's house someone had written in pencil, "Mary and Lu-seng, you have a beautiful home!" and the airy, clean, trim bamboo bungalow deserved its commendation.

Ma-ma was pleased with many observations on that visit, but a tiny incident in the evening chapel service deserves mention. Lu-seng was leading and Mary was in her usual soprano seat on the end of the first row facing the pulpit. Ma-ma was seated among the altos so that she could see both those on the platform and those in the audience. As Lu-seng warmed up to his subject he became really eloquent and Mary's face was a picture. Her soul was stirred by his message and her love for him welled up until her countenance was transfigured. Like a beautiful little opal her face glowed with adoration, fervency and devotion until suddenly his own eye saw her. For just a second, recognition of their mutual love and their heart union in the highest matters of God and man, flashed from the one to the other joyously, then just as quickly Lu-seng looked away and Mary looked down at her lap. But Ma-ma had seen.

> ". . . *When he spake and cheered his Table round*
> *With large, divine and comfortable words*
> *Beyond my tongue to tell thee—I beheld*
> *From eye to eye thro' all their order flash*
> *A momentary likeness of their King.*"

"Do you know the opal? . . . its lovely hues and that sweet lamp of fire that ever burns at its heart, for the breath of the Lord God is in it."—ELLICE HOPKINS.

And in her seat Ma-ma silently rejoiced and thanked the Lord that after five years of married life the fire still burned on;

rejoiced too that it was love of the Lord that fanned its flame higher in each heart. Such pure love had transfigured each into a "momentary likeness of the King", for no sordid passion can produce a glorified face like that; it was a light from heaven.

At the close of that visit Ma-ma had to return to Oak Flat, but not before Lu-seng had told her that he had a new idea, a new dream. He was going to tear down his new house and build an earthen house, a large two-story place which could house a hundred students or guests, sleeping sardine fashion on the floors of the upper story; also on the site of his present house he wanted to build a much larger chapel, the reason being that he wanted to bring Rainy Season Bible School over to Olives! Oak Flat had had R.S.B.S. for ten years now and the surrounding villages had had the blessings of the week-end ministry of the students. It was time the west bank of the Salween received an opportunity for such ministry. So he wished to get ready.

At that time Ma-ma had little hope of such a large move. Water and fuel were scarce at Olives, two very important items for such a large undertaking, and then a house for the missionary staff must be built—too much was involved. But Lu-seng had his vision and he proceeded to carry it out. And in one year's time, to her own astonishment, Ma-ma and her whole household were moved over to Village of the Olives, temporarily housed in Lu-seng's new home, whilst the skeleton of a bamboo shanty for her family, was going up next door! Ma-ma had two white visitors also, those busy days, one of whom was a medical doctor.

On the day that Girls' Bible School began, in February, 1949, these two much-appreciated guests left. The girls now had to take turns in preaching on Sunday noon, and it was from a message Mary gave, that Ma-ma first awakened as to the subject matter of this chapter.

"When doctor[1] was here and spoke to us," said Mary, "She helped me very much in that message on trial. I had been feeling that no one had such heavy trials as I had. But doctor said that everybody has trials and that they are purposely allowed

[1] Dr. Myrtle Jane Hinkhouse.

of God that we may develop and grow in our spiritual lives. That was a great help to me, changing my point of view. Even as a limb of the body needs exercise or it will become unusable, so we Christians must have circumstances that cast us upon God or we will never experience the strength of His undergirding arms or the faithfulness of His love towards us. That message has been a blessing to me."

Ma-ma sat up and thought. "I had been feeling that no one had such heavy trials as I had." What trials had Mary? She was hard-working for she was an industrious little body. But many other girls in Olives had to labour much harder. Lu-seng her husband was considered well off. She had to live with her in-laws but they were Christians; Rhoda was having a hard time with *her* mother-in-law, but she was a heathen, a very talkative and gossipy one. Trials? What were Mary's trials? From then on Ma-ma began to take note.

After many months of quiet alertness and putting pieces of information together, the whole matter stood revealed. This is what had happened.

For some time a silent rivalry had been growing up between the two women who loved Lu-seng supremely, his wife and his mother. Each one coveted to be dearest of all to Lu-seng, so that in family differences it must have been a problem to know which side to take, his wife's or his mother's. Little Paul was another source of rivalry (one hesitates to say jealousy, for it never reached a point of bitterness and visitors would never sense anything at all) but still it was always there, unspoken. Lu-seng-ma was what could be described as a "driver". She herself was so full of energy, worked quickly and ably. Mary, though industrious, was much slower to think or even to move. For a hint to be thrown to her husband that she had not been working hard for the family food was simply unbearable to Mary. Faithfulness was a very part of her. On the other hand, Lu-seng-ma did not mean to drive: she had a habit of talking to herself and did not realize that often she forced Mary into action when she did not know her spoken thoughts had been overheard. Mary, having lost a great deal of weight, needed no prodding to work; in fact, should have been encouraged to take things easier occasionally. But fearful lest her mother-in-law go up and down the village bemoaning that the work was not being done, Mary often forced herself into the fields when she should have rested at home. This had gone on for some six years when one day it reached a climax.

A buckwheat field waited to be harvested and Mary was feeling ill. The harvesters go into the fields with the first streaks of daylight to cut and bind by hand, with only a few minutes' rest at noon for lunch, until dark. It is very fatiguing. Mary felt that a day's delay in getting that buckwheat in would make no difference, but Lu-seng-ma, with her impatient nature, felt otherwise. She tried to hire help, but everyone was busy, she could get no one. Following her old habit unconsciously, that evening as Lu-seng-ma went up and down the trails asking for labourers she moaned out loud, "Everybody sick, just when the harvest must be brought in. It may rain and the crop be ruined. Whatever will I do. Our buckwheat for the year! And nobody will help," and so on. This was reported to Mary, as in such a small village everything is told immediately. The result was that before daylight next morning Mary, forcing herself, got up, cooked an early breakfast, and by the first streaks of light was out in the buckwheat field working hard. By night-time she was almost ready to collapse, probably vomited, when the matter came to Lu-seng's attention.

"I didn't say she had to go!" The old mother, alarmed lest she lose favour with her dear son, was on the defensive immediately. "I know she was not well and people have to rest occasionally. She *would* go." Then in a low tone to Lu-seng, "You know she is obstinate, What could I do? I couldn't tie her up, could I?" And so the argument began. It was not the first time this had happened, and Lu-seng was getting tired of it. When they were alone at night Lu-seng probably felt he should "exhort" Mary. "You're too sensitive. Don't go around with a chip on your shoulder! You know the old lady does not mean what she says. And she is right, you *are* obstinate. When she said she did not mean that you were to be the one to go harvest the buckwheat, why didn't you believe her?" and so on. Mary's only answer was a burst of tears. To Lu-seng this was disgusting weakness, and thoroughly impatient with female unreasonableness he flounced over on his bed and went to sleep.

But there was no sleep for his little wife. Every bone in her body ached from over-fatigue. But more than all her heart ached, that after trying so hard to please everybody, she had only succeeded in getting herself scolded. That Lu-seng-ma had whispered that word about obstinacy she knew right well, and she knew too the unconscious reason for it had been, not to lose favour with Lu-seng. And it was not the first time this had happened: to defend herself, the mother-in-law had blamed her, the wife, for obstinacy. Weary, discouraged and alone, the only one awake through the dark hours, the Tempter had a rare opportunity and he used it. "Put Lu-seng's love for you to the proof," he whispered. "You know what a heathen wife would do under such circumstances—run away, and stay away until he comes to fetch you. That would wake him up! And it would scare Lu-seng-ma too, for according to heathen custom, if he did not come for you within three days, your father could take him to law as not wanting you! *Does* he want you? His words to-night did not look as if he loved you—not like he used to!" The tempter of souls knows how to stir us up, and the right moment to suggest his lies. This time he succeeded. When Lu-seng got up the next morning, Mary's bed was empty. He did not think much of it, as she frequently rose before he did, but when breakfast time came and none of the family had seen her, then he became somewhat alarmed. His mother, conscience-stricken, was the first to guess what had taken place.

"Do you think she has run away?" she whispered.

Lu-seng stood transfixed. His Mary, so often pointed to by the whole village as the most faithful of wives, *run away*? Publish to everybody that his, *Lu-seng's family*, had had a quarrel? He, the most impeccable evangelist in the valley, to have such a disgrace? The fire shot to his face and his eyes blazed so that even his mother was scared. "Maybe not," she added hurriedly. "Maybe she had just gone down to her father's. I'll go right after breakfast myself. I'll tell her I was wrong and ask her to come back," she said eagerly, hoping to escape the punishment of her son's censure.

But Mary had not been seen or heard of at her father's. Alarmed, and knowing well that publicity was what Lu-seng feared more than anything else, his mother made a pretext to visit Martha, but there was no Mary there. And so on. Secretly, as long as it could be kept secret, the family hunted for Mary, but there was no trace of her. Then they had to face the inevitable; she had taken the heathen course and run away.

By now Lu-seng had himself in hand, and with his quick keen judgment he made a decision. He called the family together that evening and held a council. The first thing to be kept in mind was that this matter should not be noised abroad. He was the leading pastor of the whole church and hundreds were looking to him and his family as an example. Mary had very definitely chosen a heathen way to defend herself, but all must work together to cover up this fact if cover was at all possible. The next morning Lu-seng-pa, Lu-seng and Timothy, all making an excuse would set off in different directions to try to trace her whereabouts. One to go north, one south, and one west. It was hardly likely that she had attempted to cross the river. She was too spent physically to try to go far away. They were not to *ask* if she had run here or there; they were to inquire about grain at likely places, homes of friends, and at the same time keep their eyes open. And by the second day they had traced her—she had gone to Sandalwood Flat, to the home of Samuel Ju's mother. That old lady and Lu-seng-ma were fast friends and she had often been entertained by Mary when on a marketing trip to Olives. Mary evidently had not confided in them, merely saying that she needed a rest and had come to pay them a visit for a few days. But Samuel, a graduate of the Tali hospital, the only trained medical in the countryside, made his knowledge of how to treat sick bodies an excuse and discovered a bit of her secret. He had always been an admirer of Mary and under his kind, sympathetic questioning Mary probably relaxed and told him. Such a situation was not without danger, for Samuel was a handsome young bachelor, much desired by many maidens, but he was a Christian too and his unconcealed admiration was pleasant. So, when on the second day Timothy appeared at the Ju house, Mary knew that he was searching for her, and felt gratified that Lu-seng had not wasted any time trying to find her. She sedately refused Timothy's invitation to go home with him, saying that she wished to rest another day, and Timothy knew what that meant. There must be an invitation from Lu-seng before she would come back. But there was no scene. In fact the whole affair was a marvel of discreet and clever management, for not a breath of it ever got beyond the borders of Village of the Olives. In all such villages there are many gossips who would love such a dainty morsel that the leading pastor's wife had run away from him and he had had to send for her! That such never got abroad was miraculous; it was someone's clever and capable handling of a difficult situation. But it was managed. Two years later Ma-ma had not the faintest idea of it, not until Mary's own mention of trials set her to questioning; then Lu-seng himself finally opened up and told her.

When the little wife was brought home, according to Lisu custom, a fine chicken supper would be served; or even a pig killed to honour the occasion. Her plan seemed to have worked, the Tempter's suggestion seemed to have been just the thing. Ah, no. The Tempter never leads us into green pastures or beside still waters. Mary was to pay bitterly and for many a long day, for obeying the instincts of the flesh and the voice of God's enemy. Just a few months later came her admission in Girls' Bible School (1947) as to the blessing of Heb. 11:1, when she added, "And decision is important." Just what she meant by that none of her audience guessed, but already the bitterness of a wrong decision was beginning to eat into her life.

The first reaction in the home life of her family had been a respectful kindness shown toward her. Lu-seng had doubtless spoken to his mother, and so she went out of her way to make Mary welcome, and guarded her own tongue as she had not for a long time. But among Lu-seng's companions there was a different attitude. One of his chief friends at this time was Andrew, lately elected deacon at Olives. Andrew was brother to Lydia and married to Rhoda. They too lived with his mother and he found that his wife and parent did not get along well together. Andrew was a fine man, but naturally he sympathized with Lu-seng in the wife and mother-in-law matter; and Lydia, always an admirer of Lu-seng, was filled with resentment that Mary had almost brought the stain of public disgrace upon the young church leader. From that time on, the friendship between Mary and Lydia ceased. They spoke when necessary, but never were seen together—and formerly they were chums. On the other hand, warm-tempered Rhoda stoutly defended Mary, and carried to her all the tales of what went on when Lu-seng visited Andrew. Whether feelings were put into definite words or not, Lu-seng began to feel that Mary had injured him, and that Andrew and Lydia pitied him because of it, and his conduct began to change toward his little wife. She felt that something was gone. More and more now did Lu-seng go down the hill to Andrew's house. Sympathy and welcome awaited him there, but always, like a shadow, Rhoda flitted back and forth, and sooner or later Mary got to hear of all that had been said, or even just looked. Nothing evil took place, but Lu-seng began to make cynical, hard little remarks about wives and marriage, and he and Mary were never seen talking together. At evening chapel service the tenors and altos sat on the side, facing one another. Lu-seng was a tenor and Lydia was an alto, and so it happened that, without being conscious of it, when a fine point was made in a message, well, Lydia was right opposite and she was keen to appreciate such things, and so a smile of "That was well put. . . . Yes, wasn't it?" would flash from the one to the other. It never occurred to the young husband that Mary saw the smile and that it was like a knife in her heart. That quick fellowship with her husband in the things of God had always been one of her greatest treasures. Now her former chum had it. So many things in life we do thoughtlessly! Lu-seng and Lydia never dreamed that they had taken from Mary that which was dearer than life: probably they never gave thought to such a small matter as a smile in public. Lu-seng always had such smiles for his friends, but it just happened that Lydia sat opposite him in chapel where he could not but see her.

Ma-ma did not recognize at first what was happening. Having been on the alert to watch for Mary's troubles, she did notice that sometimes during chapel service a grim look, almost pain, would cross Mary's face, who closed her eyes for a few moments of silent prayer; gradually the tense lines would relax and peace come to her. Then she would open her eyes to fix them determinedly on the speaker, as if refusing to let outside thoughts distract. Song of Solomon 2:14, 15: "O my dove, that art in . . . the secret of the stairs . . . let me hear thy voice . . . take us the foxes, the little foxes, that spoil the vines."

Mary was learning the *secret of the stairs.*

> "*There is a viewless cloistered room,*
>   *As high as heaven, as fair as day,*
>   *Where though my feet may join the throng,*
>   *My soul can enter in and pray.*
>
> "*One hearkening even cannot know*
>   *When I have crossed the threshold o'er,*
>   *For He alone who hears my prayers*
>   *Has heard the shutting of the door.*"
>
> DOHNAVUR.

Her feet in the throng, her soul stealing quickly up the secret places of the stairs, that is how the little stone of fire endured.

What a fiery purging this experience was, one can only glimpse, never really know. A heathen wife would have replied with a flirtation; that is the Devil's way out, and there were plenty of young men who would have helped Mary quickly, if she had shown the least desire to tease Lu-seng in that way, because Olives is a large village, and has an unusual number of men, heathen as well a Christian. And Mary was notably attractive. But she had followed the Devil's advice once, and now knew that she was out reaping the harvest. Christ had a way of escape too—to let Him fill all the empty places in our hearts. She chose to try it with this heavenly Lover, to meet Him in the secret of the stairs, and confide the sorrows of her soul to His loving pure heart.

It was months before Ma-ma discovered the reason for this use of "the stairs" in chapel. Ma-ma pondered: should she speak to Lu-seng and Lydia about it? To say it was a theft—

that would be a strong word. To insinuate a smirch where no smirch had ever been would be to arouse an anger that might be hard to pacify. Bishop Taylor-Smith's words, "Sometimes to meddle is to muddle," kept ringing in her ears; and yet to know that Mary was being thus tormented in worship service, that also was hard to bear. Ma-ma found herself watching, and when she saw Mary's face grow grim and her eyes close, Ma-ma would pray also, "O Lord meet with her. Give us a solution to this." And when the look of peace ironed out the pain on that young face, Ma-ma would pray silently, "Thank Thee, Lord. Oh how wonderful Thou art." Ma-ma marvelled that this constant torment never kept Mary from chapel. Every evening, no matter how hard she had worked during the day, nor how ill she felt, she was there, and *always in her assigned place*. Stone of fire. It would have been easy to Mary to say to herself, "I won't go to service if those two keep hurting me like this," or "Well, I can sit in a different seat, where I cannot see them." She did neither. She never missed a service and never took another seat. "Passion held by principle." Unconsciously too she was learning her new lesson: worship of God and love of Lu-seng were being disentangled, permanently. Chapel service now was meeting with God, nothing else. She was allowing her soul to be tried in the fire, that it might come out pure, with only the image of the Master stamped upon it. After descending that secret stairway of prayer she opened her eyes with a resolute focusing of her attention upon the Scripture exposition, or the hymn words, and she kept them there, refusing to let them wander. Thus she grew in sweetness and power. At least two other young girls in Olives were won by Mary and nurtured up in the faith by her—Abigail and Euodia. Furthermore, during the Girls' Bible School of February, 1949, the village of Little Olives sent a message to Ma-ma after Mary had spent a week-end with them. It said: "We have received much spiritual help from this girl student: please send us more like her each week."

But the time came when Ma-ma, with a definite burden, felt that she must speak to Lu-seng about the matter. Mary was ill, the Communists were pressing down the canyon (as will be told in the following chapters) and Ma-ma knew that peace of heart must be brought to the little sick wife. She prayed for the opportunity, and one afternoon Lu-seng walked in when there was no audience.

"Lu-seng, sit down a minute" she said. "I have had something heavy on my heart to talk to you about. It weighs me down more than these political dangers; it is this matter of a rift between you and Mary. When I was here in December, 1947, I saw that there was warm love between you two and I rejoiced. Now things are different and your little wife is very sick. Samuel Ju says that Mary has been fretting about something for two years. I did not ask him what, for it is not our business. But I feel that you ought to investigate and make things right. It may be something careless that you are not conscious of, or a spoken word that hurt and which you have forgotten. There is obviously something that is causing tension and I think that it ought to be removed as soon as possible."

Lu-seng's face was sober. "I do not know of anything," he replied. "I think it is just incompatibility of temperament."

"Nothing of the sort" said Ma-ma warmly. "I do not believe it. But I think you could find out if you tried."

"Well, I certainly would want to confess it, if there was anything," said Lu-seng thoughtfully and quietly. "It would be my duty before God to do that, if for no other reason. I will go and ask." And he left the room. Ma-ma went up to her room to pray.

Later on in the day Ma-ma had reason to seek Lu-seng-ma, and so she went down the hill to the latter's house. She was not at home, but Lu-seng and Mary were. Mary lay on the plank bed by the fire, a serene smile on her face, with Lu-seng sitting close by, playing Ma-ma's victrola to her. The whole atmosphere of peace and happiness filled Ma-ma who left quickly with a prayer of thanksgiving.

Those many journeys up the secret stairway for Mary had not been in vain.

The delicate cleavage of the precious stone is not for its ruin, but for its perfect redemption.

7

Made only of Desert Dust

"Do you know that lovely fact about the opal? That in the
first place, it is made only of desert dust, sand, silica and owes
its beauty and preciousness to a defect. It is a stone with a
broken heart. It is full of minute fissures which admit air,
and the air refracts the light. Hence its lovely hues and that
sweet lamp of fire that ever burns at its heart, for the breath of
the Lord God is in it.

"You are only conscious of the cracks and desert dust, but
so He makes His precious opal. We must be broken in ourselves before we can give back the lovely hues of His light,
and the lamp in the temple can burn in us and never go out."

ELLICE HOPKINS.

MARY was ill. The first intimation of it had come during
that Christmas when the missionary lady doctor had
visited them. Mary, who as usual did the cooking for the
Christmas crowd out on a cold and windy hillside, caught a
head cold in consequence. But others were more seriously ill
in their household (both Lu-seng-pa and Timothy had to call
in the doctor's help), so she said nothing about herself. But one
day as she and her mother-in-law were beating out the corn, a
sharp pain like a knife-cut shot through her jaw and head, very
severe for a few moments; then it was gone.

Occasionally that sharp pain returned, never for long: then
in March she suddenly had a hæmorrhage from the nose and
Ma-ma was called in. Mystified, she tried different medicines
and prescribed rest. It was difficult to get rest, for Paul was sick
and cried at night, often making her get up and carry him
back and forth, even though, being four years old, he was
heavy. Also it was planting time and she must help. Thirdly,

that spring the long-threatened political upset descended upon them.

Rumours came that the Communists had arrived at Paoshan, where Ma-pa had gone *en route* to help the southern Lisu field. Then suddenly a villager who had been to Luchang to carry corn returned with the news that the Reds, about thirty of them, were already at Luchang. (One should say that these were not Reds, but brigands masquerading under that name. The Communists have since repudiated them, but all during the danger the officials in the canyon thought there might be a connection at least.) They made an attack upon Six Treasuries town, took the lairds there by surprise, captured some of their women-folk, and the lairds themselves only escaped with what they wore on their backs. These invaders confiscated everything—thousands of dollars. And last night, the rumour continued, they had arrived at Luchang and publicly said they were coming on to Olives! Everybody guessed it must be to get Ma-ma and Brother Three; no one else was worth looting except perhaps the headman Yi-hwey-pa, who had some guns.

Lu-seng came home flushed with excitement. "Mary, you and Paul must run and hide in the cave. They won't touch an old woman like mother, so she may stay. Asaph is packing up to take his wife, and Andrew is getting Rhoda out of the way. Timothy and I will help carry your rice, pots and whatever you need. I will stay home, or rather I will return home. I am going down the road to see whether these rumours are true or false. I will go toward Luchang, but I will be back by Monday night."

"Is Ma-ma hiding too?"

"No, but she has packed up some of her things and had them hidden—medicines, kerosene and such things. Maybe we are going to finish the Bible School which has begun, but—I wonder."

That year Rainy Season Bible School was held from April to June, and this occurred in the middle of the session at a week-end, when the students had scattered to far villages to preach. They were due back on Monday night. With such danger abroad, would they dare to return?

By night-time Mary and Paul, along with many of the other young women of the village, were safely hidden in a cave high up a rocky cliff, of whose existence no one else knew but the villagers. They stayed a whole week, Timothy or someone bringing them fresh supplies of food as needed. Every day it poured with rain, the streams in between Luchang and Olives rose and flooded until they were uncrossable, which was the only thing that saved them from a visit by the brigands. These had divided into two bands, one for the east bank and one for the west. The group on the east had approached young Laird Dwan at Place of Action. They demanded guns, clothing and shoes, besides much pork and liquor. He had acted very submissively, killed a pig or two, poured out keg after keg of native whiskey, made no demur when they demanded more leather shoes. Married the previous year, he had many new garments, and to his secret chagrin his own best man (Dai-yi-gwan by name) was with this group, and of course knew just what the laird possessed, even to his *seventeen pairs of leather shoes*!

They were rather surprised at his meekness, for he had a reputation for courage, but concluded that it was their unconquerable character which had quelled him. To tell the truth, Laird Dwan himself did not know whether these men were Communists or robbers, but when they began to demand so many things he quietly concluded they were the latter and made his wily plans accordingly. For a long time now he had had a Captain Tseng, hired from the soldiery disbanded at the end of the Japanese war, as his personal retainer. Unknown to anyone but Tseng, he had hand-grenades, also left over from the war, hidden behind his castle. When the brigands first arrived and asked for his guns, he had given them a couple, but only Tseng knew he had better ones concealed in another place.

All afternoon Laird Dwan acted quite humbly but chagrined. When evening fell, most of his guests, who were well under the influence of his potent liquor, went to bed to sleep heavily. After midnight, when snores and deep breathing proclaimed that all were unconscious to this world the laird tiptoed around his *yamen*, carefully locking every door but his main front one. Already secret messages had gone to all the villages within three hours' walk of his *yamen*, with the order that every Lisu who owned or could procure a gun should arrive silently at dawn next day, surround his *yamen* and shoot or capture any trying to escape by the front door! He knew the Lisu would not dare to disobey him. This laird, called Grandpa by the Lisu as a term of respect, was only twenty-three years old!

At dawn, therefore, having procured the hand-grenades from the mountainside, Captain Tseng and the laird climbed up on the roof of the *yamen* to an advantageous spot and—threw the grenades on the sleeping guests!

The carnage and pandemonium that ensued can be imagined. Remember, there is no electric light button to turn on and see what the disturbance is about.

The Lisu visitor at Lu-seng-pa's fire, who told this story, described the *yamen* as a lake of blood by the time faint daylight came to reveal the sad scene. About thirteen were dead or dying. Six, who had tried to flee through the front door, were caught by the Lisu waiting outside and tied up. The best man, Dai-yi-gwan, crept on his knees to the front threshold, presented his gun butt foremost through the opening, and cried out to the laird outside. He used the Lisu covenant name of *gwa-cho*, for he was a covenant chum of Dwan's, and that name temporarily secured his life. They said that when he was allowed to come out of that death trap, his face was ashen and he shook all over, sobbing and crying, as he flung his arms around the laird. One other was caught whose foot was so badly shattered that he cried for death and swallowed opium.

"What will Grandpa do now?" questioned Mary. "He would not dare to sleep in the *yamen* after all those people died there! That would be *chya* to him." *Chya* is laying oneself open to the demons' revenge and can only be overcome by animal sacrifice and incantation.

"He says he is going to move over to Olives," said the visitor. "The runner who brought this news prepared us. Yi-hwey-pa must make arrangements to receive the laird's household. His women arrive tomorrow. They are sleeping in Beheaded Tribesman Village to-night. In fact, they had already taken refuge there before these brigands got to Place of Action."

"*Ai-ya*" groaned Lu-seng-ma. "If the laird moves over here, then we'll be bothered greatly. Messages have to be taken for him day and night. All his poor relations have to be fed, and they will go out at night and filch corn and beans from our fields. *Ai-ya*, that is bad news for us. Why does he have to come to Olives?"

"Because he is afraid of revenge. If these men are Communists, then the Reds in the Mekong Valley will come over the hill and take revenge. Grandpa wants the Salween River between him and them. And all rope bridges over the Salween have to be cut except the one at the bottom of this village. The order has gone forth already. Then no one can get here unless they cross our bridge. The river is already so high that rafts would perish. The rains are very early this year you know."

Mary and Paul were home again now, for the brigands had suddenly left. The laird's victory had given a sense of security, while the Chinese magistrate had skipped over the mountain into Burma, hired a group of Kachin army men who had good rifles, and with these he was attempting to encircle the brigands. This made them retire to the eastern bank where they cut the Luchang rope bridge. Rope bridges cannot be made in the flood season; once cut, the crossing is hopeless until autumn, when the river goes down low enough for a raft to venture over, carrying the end of the new bridge to be tied to that bank.

So the next day it happened just as the visitor had said—a long line of refugees were seen coming up from the Olives rope bridge. Early that morning the towncrier had gone calling orders. "A man or woman from each house to the rope bridge immediately! We must help carry the women and things of the laird's household up from the river."

Low murmurs of resentment were his only response, but no one dared refuse. Lu-seng was studying in the Bible School still, for all the students had returned; Mary was not strong enough to carry such heavy loads now; Lu-seng-pa and the mother were both over sixty years, too old to carry; so that left Timothy as the only one to represent their family. If Timothy carried for the laird, Mary must watch the cows, for oxen, which are indispensable to ploughing those steep and rocky hillsides, must be carefully herded or they fall over the cliffs. As Mary opened the door under Lu-seng-ma's shanty, for the cows to come out, she could see the path up from the rope bridge to the village. The east side of Olives rises in an abrupt ridge of rock which juts up perpendicularly making the village into an oval bowl, but at its south end falls away suddenly, leaving a passage between the ridge and the mountain proper. Through this defile, with its background of mountainside towering up across the river, slips the trail from the village down to the river bank. Already a long single file was laboriously ascending. The laird's wife, her mother, her mother's other children, the laird's brothers and sisters which numbered five or six, and various cousins, slaves, servants and soldiers were climbing up into the village. Two or three rode horses, the laird's wife and mother-in-law must ride a mountain chair, which is equivalent to a sedan chair carried on men's shoulders, and the villagers of Olives must leave their field work and do the carrying free of charge. They were serfs. Mary could make out Abigail, Susanna and some of the other girls bent over with the heavy load put upon their backs, labouring up the slope below. They looked like bent pins and the horses like pinheads crawling up in between the great craggy rocks. Mary sighed, but at least she was glad that the laird's party were going to stay at the north end of the dell—that was almost a mile away from the chapel. It was better than next-door or in their midst.

That night when she returned home Timothy was talking about it. "This is only the beginning," he growled. "Grandpa himself comes to-morrow and all his soldiers and retinue! They have already been to borrow our tables. We can eat on the floor, of course. *They* must have tables. Yi-hwey-pa figures there will be seventy of them when they are all here. Seventy people to find food for twice a day!"

"But our village does not have to supply all that," put in old Lu-seng-pa. "Runners have already gone to inform the villages around how much each has to bring of beaten-out rice and beans."

"Yes?" drawled Timothy. "And who are the runners? We

are. Running on his errands day and night now, carrying our own food."

"And it is farming time," moaned Lu-seng-ma. "Mary is sick and there is only Timothy. If he sends Timothy, what will we do?"

"When R.S.B.S. is over I will go sometimes," said Lu-seng comfortingly. And this conversation was being repeated in every hut in the village that night. Entertaining Grandpa is a well-known affair in Lisuland and it is not enjoyed either.

The next morning at daylight the town-crier was again plodding up the mountain to his post in the middle of the village beside Ma-ma's house, and once more his voice rang out harshly, "One man from every house to go to the rope bridge! The laird and his men to cross to-day!" And once more a trickle of grumbling sleepy men and women, their carrying yokes slung over their shoulders, started down the trail. That afternoon as R.S.B.S. was dismissed, Ma-ma spied the long single file climbing up to the dell. The laird and several men were riding bare-back; they had not taken time to find their harness. Lu-seng, standing beside Ma-ma, said in disgust, "Now our village becomes the focus of attention from the Reds or brigands or whatever they are. If they don't make him pay for that midnight massacre, I'm mistaken."

Jonah, his load delivered and so free to go home, passed them on his way up the mountain. "He brought over those six men he captured in his *yamen* that night. Says he's going to kill them to-morrow."

"Oh no!" cried out Ma-ma. "Oh why does he have to do that? Why didn't he do it before crossing the river? Why do we have to witness such a thing?"

"Well, maybe it was only talk," said Jonah quickly, seeing that Ma-ma was very upset.

"Is Dai-yi-gwan, his best man, among them?" asked Ma-ma.

"No; he is dead. The laird told him that if he would behave himself and not try to escape he would spare him and even give him fifty dollars to get home. But a group of armed men have arrived at Be-heh over the mountain from the *yamen*; they came from the Mekong, and Dai-yi-gwan ran away at dawn to join them and lead them in against the laird, I suppose. Anyway he was missed; the laird sent two soldiers after him to shoot him on sight, which they did on the mountain pass."

"Oh I do hope there is going to be no killing here," moaned Ma-ma.

"Maybe it was just talk, Ma-ma. Don't worry," said Jonah kindly, passing on to his mud house at the top of the village.

But Ma-ma could not get rid of the horror of it. She went to seek Brother Three, for Ma-pa was still out in Paoshan, now besieged, people said, by this same group.

Brother Three thought carefully. To go himself and ask to see them the moment they arrived in the village might be to throw suspicion on himself, for it was still being whispered that these men were Communists, and in any case the affair was political. Finally, Brother Three decided to ask one of the R.S.B.S. students who had studied Chinese in the church school and Teacher Jeremiah, who had picked up Chinese whilst living in Paoshan for some months at one time, and send them down to Hanna's house where the prisoners were quartered, to see if an opportunity might not be given them to speak. They went on Saturday morning early before their week-end assignments (for Rainy Season Bible School was in session, you remember) and before noon they were back, their faces shining with joy.

"Oh Ma-ma!" they cried. "The prisoners were delighted! We explained the way of salvation to them and read some verses from the Bible. They understood our Chinese and four accepted the Lord! The two older men laughed, but four are young—three of them about sixteen years of age—and the four said that they were 'pleased to death,' and they thanked us bending their knees and knocking their heads on the ground to us!"

"Praise the Lord," said Ma-ma.

"After a while I will go and see them myself," added Brother Three, "and teach them further if it is allowed," which promise he kept.

"The youngest boy knows Ma-pa. He asked if Ma-pa is in the village now. He says Ma-pa stayed at his uncle's inn often and preached to him, but he did not pay any heed to him then. He is sorry now."

"Was there any talk of execution?" asked Ma-ma.

"No; they aren't even tied up. Hanna cooked breakfast for them this morning."

But at noon there was a sound of shots. Mary and Lois ran quickly along the upper trail and saw that the six men had been lined up in the middle of the dell. The laird ordered his soldiers to shoot a certain three, whilst the other three shattered in nerves and weeping, were led back to Hanna's house. One of the three dead was that youngest boy. It was horrible. Everyone in the village felt upset.

"And I expect he will make us bury them!" said Lu-seng fiercely; which he did. Abigail's mother and two men villagers were ordered to dig a deep hole in a field nearby; one of the diggers was bribed to cut out the tongues of the dead so that they might not be able to tell God who had killed them! A man clever enough to capture his captors was yet so blinded by superstition as to think he could fool the God of the universe as to who had slain these poor, misguided children.

"Why did he kill the young ones?" moaned Ma-ma.

"He says that when they first arrived at his *yamen* they swaggered in front of him, brandished their revolvers at him, and he decided then, in his heart, to get even," replied Lu-seng grimly.

"Then that is why God let him bring them over here," Ma-ma mused. "I should rejoice and not be so upset. It was that they might hear the Word of Life before they were hurried into eternity. Man would not give them a second chance, *but God did*. Oh, how grateful we ought to be that we did not delay in attempting to teach them the way of salvation! And how good to be God's man in God's place!" Ma-ma was still unnerved and heart-sick over the pitiable affair, but this thought was some comfort to her.

Lu-seng and Timothy were both under orders now from the laird to take messages across the river to Cow's Hump Village. He needed two men to go, and as it was the week-end Lu-seng offered, thinking to minister the gospel to the Christians there on the Lord's Day before returning. They were commissioned to bring back a report of what the laird's spies across the river had discovered concerning that band of armed men just over the eastern mountain-tops.

Lu-seng came back grinning.

"I'm glad we are not rich!" he chuckled. "There was Sa-si-nyio-pa's family in awful trouble. Everyone in Cow's Hump has gone into hiding, because they fear an attack. One man in each family sneaks back in the daytime to see if everything is all right, otherwise the village is deserted. They are living in caves and small booths in the woods, or anywhere. But rich Sa-si-nyio-pa, possessing bushels and bushels of grain! Where could he hide it? No one could ever carry it all to a cave, and, if there is no attack, back again! And his pork hams!" Again that merry chuckle. "About ten of them were dangling around his head while he stood in the midst of his many belongings and shouted orders, and countermanded them, and his family scurried here and there grabbing this and finding it too heavy to carry and then dropping it, while Sa-si-nyio-pa shouted again and mopped his brow!" By this time Mary and the whole family were in laughter. "It is true what the Bible says, 'Go to now, ye rich men, weep and howl for your miseries that shall come upon you.'"

"Did anyone come to service?" Mary asked.

"Yes; they came back when they heard I had arrived. But it is true that there are armed men at Be-heh—there are about one hundred there. Spies go and come all the time."

"Grandpa has bought two machine guns from Tengchung," quietly put in old Lu-seng-pa. "His youngest brother has gone to get them and is expected here to-morrow—two villagers have been ordered to help carry them."

About ten days later, at dusk, the town-crier ascended to the middle of the village, crying, "A man from each house must go to Ba-ju-de and guard all night. Fifty men have been seen advancing on us! One man from each house go!" A muttered storm of remonstrance was his answer. That day every villager had been labouring in the corn-fields hoeing for some thirteen hours, only stopping long enough to eat lunch. They had just returned home when this order came, and it was raining, the steady, regular pat-pat of a whole night of rain in the rainy season. But Grandpa's orders may not be questioned, and after a leisurely meal the poor, tired fellows were seen going down the trail, crossbows over their shoulder, long knives hanging from their belts, no protection from the wet but a big straw hat. At breakfast-time Mary saw Timothy walk into their shanty and throw himself wearily on the bed.

"All for nothing," he said shortly. "It was just a bunch of traders from Tengchung. Now that all the rope bridges are cut across the Salween the only place anyone can cross is our village. They are a ragged, pitiful bunch, those traders. They will be here shortly. All their profit in trade has been spent in food for these days of delay in getting home, and some have had to sell their clothes already; and after they get across our rope bridge they will still have over a week's journey to walk—and eat."

And then began a long line of refugees coming to Olives, among whom were a group of Tibetans. The rope bridge had to be guarded night and day now, and the Lisu must do that also. Each home must send one man for four days and nights of watching. Lu-seng-pa was able to do this, so Timothy could be spared for the farm work. The armed men across the eastern mountains were reported to be getting ready to attack, so Laird Dwan took his young captain and went personally into the mountains to supervise a barricade. The Lisu on the eastern bank had to watch all the trails into the canyon from Be-heh night and day, so those of Olives knew that they were not the only ones who were suffering for lack of time on their fields.

Lu-seng-ma had a new grievance. The laird had decided to fortify the western bank at the rope bridge of Olives, and he ordered trenches dug round it. That plot of land was Lu-seng-ma's cotton-field, but it was dug up without even consulting her and with no remuneration. All their planted cotton, the family's new clothes for next year, gone at one sweep—and for nothing, for no attack was ever made.

Then one day a long line of people were discerned coming down the eastern bank from the north—about thirty-seven— but there being no binoculars in Olives, no one knew just who they were, but an attack on the rope bridge was suspected. The Communists had already entered the canyon to the north and

won over to their side the local schoolmaster, who happened
to be a Christian of the northern church, a young man named
Thomas, whom Ma-ma designated Red Thomas to distinguish
him from Homay's husband. Red Thomas had sent messages that
the Reds were planning to come down and "liberate". Was that
long single file of silent people the advance guard of the Communist army? Once more the weary farmers were called to
leave their beds and go down to guard at the river bank. And
once more it proved for naught. Morning light revealed that
the thirty-seven were Lisu salt-carriers, many of them women,
who were trying to get across the Salween and carry salt from
the salt wells in the Mekong Valley to Tengchung, where the
price was high. The laird happened to be returning and met
this group and—refused to let them cross. He had also planned a
salt trade with Tengchung and wishing to keep the price up, he
told them at the river brink that they might not cross. All their
poor little funds were sunk in the salt on their backs. They begged
to be allowed to sell it to villagers of Olives, many of whom
now had no salt at all, but the laird refused. Villagers of Olives
could buy from him, at his price, in a day or so when his horses,
carrying salt, arrived. The poor Lisu. They had just descended
two thousand feet of unusually steep mountain; now they must
retrace it with their heavy loads, and many of them were
women. To force women to carry over one hundred pounds
of salt up a climb so steep that one's knees came near one's chin,
and two thousand feet high! It was iniquitous. The only alternative was to sell to the laird at almost cost price and go home
empty, with no cloth for the children's winter clothes, as they
had hoped to obtain. Many sold to the laird rather than injure
their bodies for life with such a climb and such loads. And the
laird forced the villagers of Olives to drag the salt across the rope
bridge and carry it to his house, without wages! Later when his
own horse-loads of salt arrived, Olives villagers had to toil
unremittingly for two days, carrying his salt from the river
bank to his house, a fifteen-hundred-foot climb! Every house
had to be represented, and they must continue to carry until
all the salt was up. Many of the girls had to carry several times
in the day. And the only reward—the privilege of buying some

from him *at the usual price*! There was no other salt to be had.

During these days of high-pressure living, Mary's trouble from her nose got worse and hæmorrhages occurred not only every day, but several times a day. None of Ma-ma's efforts or Samuel Ju's was of any avail. When at length she got very weak —for two weeks on end she had lost much blood every day— Ma-ma, in growing anxiety, suggested that they have an anointing service over her. While the group in evening chapel prayed, the deacon, Ma-pa and Brother Three anointed her. Ma-pa was now back. The bleeding stopped, except for once the next day and then none at all. How everyone rejoiced! Even the heathen had been in great concern, for this little stone of fire, so long taken for granted in the community, was missed to a degree that surprised them. Lu-seng was amazed at the earnest inquiry from heathen. And this was a chance to testify to what the Lord alone could do. But strength had gone and it would be a long time before Mary could do normal work. No one spoke of it, but it was Lu-seng now who herded the cows, and it was impossible for him to make his pastoral visits.

In August another sick one drew the focus of attention from Mary. The white missionary at Mya-Goo, Sister Four,[1] had taken seriously ill. A runner came in with letters from her husband, Oldest Brother, telling of her dangerous complications and sufferings, which only hospitalization could relieve. At length she begged to be sent down to Ma-ma and perhaps later get to the hospital in Chinaland. Oldest Brother could not accompany her, for they had three small children, and their Rainy Season Bible School was in session; so the runner had come saying that Sister Four had started out alone with the Lisu, and would Brother Three come up the canyon and escort her? He left early the next morning. There followed a few days of concerned waiting before another runner arrived with the news of an accident in a Lisu hut which had increased her suffering; and she had run out of powdered milk: would someone please bring some? The letter came as dusk and rain were falling, but two R.S.B.S. students offered to go all night in spite of the very serious danger of falling rocks, if they could have a lantern to

[1] Leila Cooke.

see the way! Two lanterns were provided and the brave boys started out, whilst the ones at home prayed. Every now and again the ominous sound of rocks tearing out of the softened soil above them and crashing down the mountainside over their path was heard. Not knowing where the rocks would hit, they stood and prayed, but God saw them through and the precious missionary's life was saved. Two days later she was carried on a stretcher into Olives.

Although confined to bed the whole time she was in Olives (for the appendix burst after she arrived), Sister Four's life among them was a blessing they will often talk about. She was so interested in them. By this time Mary was able to walk, and as she came shyly in to see the white woman invalid, they had sweet fellowship together. Sister Four, for all her suffering, was very observant.

"Mary is a nice girl," she commented to Ma-ma. "She ought to get medical care. If she is well enough to walk now, why not let her go out with me to Paoshan city to the Holy Light Clinic there? When Oldest Brother and the children arrive in October to take me out, I will take Mary with me."

This kind suggestion gave Mary a new lease of life. Ma-ma had studied all the medical books in the station and come to the conclusion that Mary had a polypus in her nose. Ma-ma had never heard of polypus before, but Sister Four had. "I knew a man who had one," she said. "It is not very serious and can be removed quite easily. Yes, Mary must go out with me; I will have two Lisu girls with me to care for the children, so Mary will have companions." Ma-ma asked Mary if she would ride in a mountain chair like Sister Four, but Mary would not hear of it. No Lisu would ride such, except they were unconscious, or at least too weak to stand. Nobody knew that Mary had anything more than a polypus, and even if they had, she would not have accepted a chair. That would be "hunting glory"; in other words, placing oneself on a par with the laird's wife. The Lisu despise a native who seeks to elevate himself above his station in life, and can be very stubborn about it.

Then there was great talking in Lu-seng-ma's house. Mary to go to the big Chinese city! No other girl in Olives had been there, but the men who carried Ma-pa's flour and sugar in had brought many tales of its wonders, of the shops and the glitter of things on the big markets! Lu-seng had been; and Timothy, without consulting anyone, had asked Oldest Brother if he might go and carry Sister Four's loads, and he had been accepted! Usually quiet and submissive in the home, this time Timothy asserted himself. He had never been to the big city and now he was going—no matter what! Well, that was a comfort to Mary, for Timothy was just like a brother. Ma-ma said she would pay for Mary's food and expenses and so it was settled. Hope burned high; Mary began to eat better and put on a little weight, and everyone was interested and praying for her. Ma-ma was coming out later, for she had contracted an eye disease in treating the villagers, and her eyes had never been quite the same since. The laird's strong stand against the silent Communists in the Mekong seemed to have been effective: the countryside was peaceful. Now was the time to go out for medical attention. Ma-ma, having lent her mule to Oldest Brother, would wait until it came back; then she and Danny would also come to Paoshan.

So in high spirits the caravan started out. Though it was a pull to leave little Paul, Mary did not weep at parting as much as she had feared, she might. The carriers, boys from Olives, helped to make the trip enjoyable, even though it rained for several days. Having small children in the party they could not make very long stages, and the walking through new countrysides with merry Olives boys was interesting. Being harvest-time, they saw many Chinese and Nosu tribespeople cutting grain and sleeping in the fields in improvised shelters. Then what was Mary's amazement, on leaving the Burma Road, to see the familiar life-on-the-perpendicular fall away into flat plain country—life-on-the-horizontal. *Ah-beh! Ah-beh!* She and the other Lisu girls would cry at the sight of miles of level land, the beautiful, mountain-skirted Paoshan plain.

Even before they reached the plain, while walking the Burma Road, they heard a queer sound, honk-honk, and a house on wheels came whizzing by! This was their first view of a truck; "mo-to-cah" they heard was its name! Oh what would it be like to ride one! Eagerly the Lisu carriers asked: how much would it cost to ride? Would they let Lisu ride? Not one of them but would have given some of his precious wages for a chance to get on that house with wheels! However, when they reached the edge of the plain they saw another kind of vehicle, a horse cart! This they hired for Sister Four, Mary and the children, so that they might ride into the city. Oh what fun, but rather alarming too, for it jolted over the rough road squeaking and whining, so that Mary held on tight lest it collapse. And the thousands of people! This little maid from the mountains had never seen more than a few hundred together: the six hundred at Christmas festival would be reckoned few among the teeming hundreds of this plain. She remembered Lu-seng's description of the many people in Chinaland, and there came a tug at her heart as she wondered how long she would have to wait before she saw her dear, quiet shanty home again. Where were the carriers, those familiar Olives faces? She tried to look back, but could not discern them. Arriving at the city, she was impressed with those monstrous gates and feudal city wall! She saw soldiers guarding them. Now they must descend and walk, over the cobblestone street lined on either side with those shops Lu-seng spoke of, full of beautiful, glittering things. The little mountain maid was dazzled into silence. Suddenly a soldier came from a tiny square hut, pointing his gun at them he demanded, "What people?" Terrified Mary and the nearest Lisu girl shrank to-gether but Oldest Brother not the least afraid, calmly answered in Chinese, "Americans" and walked past. Entering a tiny narrow alley they knocked at a door in a high wall. As she passed through it Mary found herself in the most beautiful garden she had ever seen, with a Chinese house, something like the laird's, only smaller, in the background. The missionary who landscaped and planted it herself came running out to greet them, and as the white people shook hands, an old, kindly Chinese man beckoned to the Lisu and led the way to their quarters—Mary and the girls were in an upper room above the native kitchen.

Before dark noises below proclaimed the arrival of the other carriers and one said in dear, familiar Lisu, "Where are we going to sleep?" Mary looked out to see the boys from Olives, putting down their loads, their long trek over, the joy of spending their wages looming up close. Mary, soon in their midst, greeted them as if she had not seen them for a year, and everyone talked of the wonders of Chinaland and what they meant to buy! She intended buying some good cloth for a suit for Lu-seng, a bright cap for Paul and a mirror for herself! And so they talked around their open wood fire, as happy a group as you would find.

The next day Sister Four said that Mary was to go with her to the Clinic. A white doctor examined Mary's nose, announced that it *was* a polypus, but as he did not have the proper instrument he could not remove it. First Mary must be built up physically; she must wait also until Ma-ma and Danny came out to Paoshan, when they would discuss the next step. After a blood test, she was given a tonic and Oldest Brother saw to it that she had good food, expensive though it was. The Clinic was like a labyrinth to Mary with its halls, courtyards, white-robed nurses and smell of medicines. She was glad to get out into more open spaces where she could see the sky. But her purchases must be made to-day for the Olives boys were leaving shortly, as they could not afford to stay too long in the expensive city, and she must have her things ready for them to carry back. Timothy and Solomon went with her down the crowded market-places. The cloth was plentiful, but oh, the price! As each stall calmly stated the cost, Mary's face fell. "I could get it cheaper at home, from the merchants who come from Burma?" she consulted with Timothy. "Yes; you could. Lu-seng will understand," comforted Timothy. So she bought the cap for Paul and the mirror and some other things, and by that time was strangely weary. There was so much to look at, it was bewildering, and then the constant hum of that unknown tongue, Chinese! She was glad to get back to her loft over the kitchen and lie down.

The next day came the separation. Such a hustle and bustle of the tribesboys getting their loads tied up to start the homeward trek! That large iron pot, so useful in the little mountain shanty, was such an unhandy shape to get into a back basket! That earthenware jar, just the thing for pickles, and not obtainable in the mountains; would not the wife rejoice to see it, and it only cost forty cents. But how to pack it so that it would not break? And then these shoes and red stockings for the children:

they must not get near the sooty cooking pot or their beauty will be ruined. And so on. To an unacquainted onlooker they are a torn, dishevelled, ragged, noisy lot. But to the white Ma-ma who has lived among them and shared their joys and sorrows, and seen their poverty and their brave courage, it is easy to be patient and hard to say goodbye. Sister Four's eyes filled with tears when bidding goodbye to them whose shoulders were still sore from carrying her and her loads.

"*Hwa-hwa!* I wish I were going back with you," she said. And little Mary, standing near, had a sudden desolation sweep over her. They were going, her friends from Olives, and she was to stay behind! In a week's time they would be at Olives, coming in around the long curve, and up the trail beside Mark's house, and they would see her little Paul and——Oh she must go back with them too! But no, orders were otherwise.

"We are keeping Solomon behind to help us with the children, so you will have one Lisu that you know nearby to talk to," said Oldest Brother kindly.

Everybody was kind but oh, to return to the loft over the kitchen and find no Lisu girls there now, and to look down the ladder and see only Solomon mending the fire! Oh, it was a terrible feeling. During the day the Chinese Christian boy, who when off duty cooked for Li Ma-pa, came and sat down beside Solomon.

"I want you to teach me Lisu," he said. "I like the Lisu of whom Eva Tseng has told me. I study the Bible each evening with Li Ma-pa, and when they have to go on furlough my wife and I will not be working here and wish to come to Lisu-land and be Chinese home missionaries to the Lisu!"

"Thank you to death!" answered Solomon, pleased and flattered that a Chinese would want to learn anything from him. "I'll be glad to teach you Lisu." And there followed lots of laughter, and a short lesson in "Come and eat" and such phrases. Everyone was as kind as could be, but Mary's heart became more and more homesick. Each day in thought she travelled with those returning carriers. At the end of the week, the day they were due to arrive in Olives, it seemed as if she had been in Chinaland a year. How *could* she endure it? It would still be a few days before Ma-ma and Danny could get ready to start, no doubt, and then it would be another week before they even arrived at Paoshan, and after that maybe they would take her still farther away to a hospital and—she would have died of this ghastly homesickness by that time!

"I want to go home," she confided in Solomon. "They say they cannot take out the polypus here. What is the use of my waiting? There is the buckwheat to be gathered in at home, and the winter's spinning, and I just sit around here every day and do nothing. Tell Oldest Brother that you and I are going home?"

"Made only of desert dust." The little stone of fire had lost her shine. Her whole soul seemed to have been engulfed in a panic of homesickness.

"Oh, she may not go home now," Oldest Brother remonstrated to Solomon. "Ma-ma is just about to start. She will be here in just a few days, and then Mary can consult with her and perhaps get to a hospital."

Back went Solomon with the white man's message, but Mary's mouth set grimly.

"I have no assurance that Ma-ma will take me to the hospital at Tali. Tell him I want to go home, and maybe I can come out again next spring—perhaps Lu-seng would bring me. I'm wasting time here. I want to go."

Rather shamefacedly Solomon went back to talk again with Oldest Brother.

"Why, Solomon, Ma-ma has already started out. It is just a matter of a few days now. Exhort her to be patient. Isn't she having good things to eat? She is getting stronger with this tonic and the meat each day; she's not wasting time. Besides, it would not be proper for you and for her to travel a week's journey alone together! She *must* stay. If she is bound to go, then let her wait until Ma-ma comes and she can return with Ma-ma's carriers."

> "To live within the present tense
> And show a heavenly glimpse of blue
> To all with whom I have to do"

yes, that is what a stone of fire should do. But—

"Within an unknown land
Alone where no familiar thing
May bring familiar comforting"

what are you going to do then? Principle had gone over-
board, only passion, a great strong upsurging desire to get
home and get little Paul into her arms once more had taken
possession of her. What if she were gone so long that little
Paul refused to come to her, as he had to his father? What if
he only loved his grandmother now? Mary's mouth set.

"Solomon, I've got to go. Please don't desert me. I can't
live another day down here. I'm going to-morrow. Tell him
so. I'm sorry to offend him, he has been so good to me, but he
does not understand how I feel inside. I don't understand it
myself. I can't explain. I just know *I've got to go*!"

And loyal Solomon, ashamed and yet obedient, went back
to Oldest Brother and gave her ultimatum. Oldest Brother and
Sister Four could hardly believe their ears. "I never met anyone
so obstinate in all my life!" Oldest Brother later told Ma-ma.
And when they finally, Solomon and Mary, appeared packed
to go, the next morning, Oldest Brother was so annoyed that
he refused to shake hands. He thought perhaps that might change
them, for the white missionary's displeasure is a very terrible
stigma in Lisuland. But it didn't, and the pair of them, Solomon
carrying her bundle and his, started off on foot for the long trek
home. Oldest Brother and Sister Four were really alarmed. It
was Lu-seng's wife and it was not proper. The only thing they
could do now was to pray. And so down on their knees they got
and asked God somehow to stop that couple, somehow to save
Mary from the disgrace she was too blind to discern. And God,
in His pity, answered as only God could.

Ma-ma and Danny had had a lovely trip out. The weather
was perfect, and gloriously invigorating as only autumn in the
mountains can be. The joy of harvest, the stacks of ripened
grain being hauled into the homes of the people, the sense of
plenty which comes with that season of the year, the deep blue
skies, the golden fields, the crisp air—how good it was to be
alive!

The morning they struck the motor road they made good time, and hearts were merry, for Ma-ma had promised that if they met an empty truck going to Paoshan she would pay half their fare if they would pay the other half, and that brought it into possibility for each of them. About half-past ten in the morning as they were rounding a sharp curve with mountains striking straight up from their right and falling precipitously away from their left, one of them stopped and said. "Sh! I heard a halloo and it sounded like Mary's voice!" Immediately everyone stopped and turned toward the mountain bank at their right. "Ho-o-o!" Yes, someone was calling them. Everyone started to search the wild mountainside with their eyes, and there, right near the top, they discerned a tiny thread of a trail and on it two human figures, no bigger in size than a pin-head. But again came the voice, this time calling a name, "Mark-k-k!" "It's Mary and Solomon!" Mark exclaimed excitedly. "They must be going home! The trail for Olives leaves the motor road just fifteen minutes' walk from here!"

"Hi!" he called back. "Come down and talk to us. Ma-ma's here! What are you doing?"

"It's too far to go back," came Mary's voice again, but they had seen her stop and talk with Solomon. "Unless Ma-ma promised to take me to Tali Hospital!"

Well, a conversation back and forth up and down five hundred feet of mountain is not very satisfactory.

"I can't promise to take her there," said Ma-ma. "Didn't she go with Sister Four? Didn't Sister Four go to the hospital? I do not know what happened in Paoshan after the carriers returned. Try to get Mary down here."

"I know," said Samson. "Tell them to come back to the noon eating place; it is just down the trail from them and only fifteen minutes' walk for us." So Mark shouted this suggestion back. The group on the road saw the two pin-points on the high trail again in consultation. Then came Solomon's voice, "Mary's coming! I'll wait here. We've already eaten lunch."

Then the pin-points separated, one running back over the slender trail and soon lost from sight by bushes and the other sitting down to wait patiently.

A few more curves and Ma-ma's group arrived at the noon stopping place: one lone hut by the side of the Burma Road, but a clear stream nearby provided water, and plenty of dead sticks on the wild mountainside supplied fuel. Soon little fires were gleaming here and there, and the clank of copper cooking kettles and the swish of rice being washed filled the air pleasantly. Soon there was a "Coo-ee" from the trees above and Mary dropped down the steep trail and ran up to shake hands. Ma-ma thought she had never seen Mary look so beautiful. She was much plumper than when she left home, her cheeks were pink with healthy exercise, and her face was wreathed in happy smiles at meeting fellow villagers once more. Her lovely teeth gleamed like pearls as she ran up joyously to this and that "brother" to shake hands, until she came to little Danny, who was Paul's playmate at home. Then the long pent-up homesickness found a vent and the tears fell. "I'm so homesick for Paul," she explained, wiping the wet off her face, "and the sight of Danny brought it back."

While the rice cooked, Mary sat down by the fire at the side of the road and told her story. The doctor had not thought that Sister Four needed to go to the hospital, at least for a few months. And he could not operate on her polypus because he had no instrument in the clinic. Then she told, quite frankly, of her unbearable homesickness and how she and Solomon had started out. Already the change from the confines of the city to the wild free life of the mountains had done her a lot of good. She was much more open to reason.

"Mary," said Ma-ma to her, drawing her aside so they could talk privately, "You know you left a note behind for me, when you left with Sister Four. And it contained most interesting news. I have told nobody, as you asked, but stop and think a moment. You said the baby is due next March. How can you think of coming out again another time for the polypus operation? Once your baby is in your arms you are a prisoner at home—you cannot travel. To me it seems as if it is now or never for your operation?"

Mary flushed, but did not wait long to answer.

"All right, Ma-ma," she said. "I will go back with you if

you want me to. But Solomon says he can't be bothered walking that road again. There is a village up over the trail and he says he will wait there until your carriers return, then join them, and they can all go back together." So God answered prayer.

Mary was a different girl. To walk with the dearly beloved brethren of Olives and get all the village news. To hear that Paul had not forgotten her, that he longed for her, was delighted with his new cap, and would wear no other; to hear that Lu-seng had gone off to Burma, driving their refractory old bull to market, hoping to sell him for a good price and bring back a more manageable one and also medicines and things for the family. It was all as water to a thirsty soul; she did not notice the miles of road that they were walking.

As it began to grow late, Ma-ma announced a stop. "To-morrow is Sunday and we will just spend it here, so watch for a good place to camp!" The carriers looked at one another. Nobody wanted to stop a day so close to the great city, yet not in it! "It is not far to Paoshan now," one suggested gently. "We could get up early and be in for the noon service?"

"Yes, but there is no need to do that," Ma-ma expostulated. "There is a village over that hill where they understand a bit of Lisu; I have slept there before—years ago. We can witness to them to-morrow. Everybody passes them by, anxious, like you, to get to the city. No, we stay here tommorow." But God took it out of Ma-ma's hands.

A truck came whirling down the road. Now, a truck would take them into the city in just two hours, and Ma-ma's promise of help with the expense of riding still could be claimed. Some of the Lisu held out their hands hopefully, but the truck swung by as if without eyes. However, when it got to the bottom of the hill it unexpectedly pulled up, stopped, and two men got out! Immediately the Lisu pelted down the slope hoping that, at the last moment, they would get the desire of their hearts, a truck ride, and into the city on Saturday night to boot. Ma-ma saw them talking with the two men, then the whole crowd turned and pelted back as hard as they could run.

"The driver says he will take Ma-ma and Danny and one other—he has not room for more! Oh, Ma-ma, you know I've

never been on a truck!" came from several panting throats at
once.

Ma-ma was taken aback. She had seen that the truck could
not accommodate all of them and mentally had decided to let
these anxious youngsters have their longings satisfied, send
them on ahead, and she herself come along on Monday.

"No," they said. "The driver is a Christian, he says, and he
knows Li Ma-ma, and he will take only you and Danny and
one other, as we told you!"

Whom to take? Never was Ma-ma in a harder place than when
she faced those eleven pairs of longing eyes. "It must be someone who knows Li Ma-ma's house," she answered slowly. Then
as her eye fell on the Lisu maiden, "I'll take Mary." And the
decision was made. Somehow Mary had never expected it.
Always in Lisuland men come first and it was the habit of her
life to expect to be only after them. You should have seen the
way her face lit up as the truth dawned on her, until she fairly
radiated excitement and joy. Ma-ma and Danny were being
ushered in to a seat in the cab, a kind Chinese gentleman re-
linquishing his own for it, he having to stand on the footguard
in consequence. Mary was told to climb up behind, but, being a
mountaineer, that presented no difficulties; so soon, with shining
eyes, and a wave of the hand at her comrades who were left so
quickly by the side of the road, the truck was off.

Never in her life had she been swung so swiftly through
space, as she was now. What had taken her and Solomon many
hours to traverse was covered before dark! The truck stopped
some distance short of the city, but the kind Chinese Christian
procured a horse-cart to take them, and paid the whole price
of it himself! He was a refugee himself from Peking during the
Japanese war, he told Ma-ma and he was now trying to earn
money to finish his education. He had been a Christian only a
year or so. As he had to get off at his school he gave many
instructions to the horse-cart driver how to care for the party
before he himself descended. Now it was late at night, for the
cart did not travel at the speed of the truck. But eventually
Mary steered Ma-ma and Danny through the dark streets,
nudged Ma-ma when the sentry challenged them, told her what

to answer, and got them all safely into Li Ma-pa's compound.

What excitement when the household learned who had arrived! "Wherever did you meet Mary?" asked Sister Four wrapping her housecoat snugly around her as she came downstairs. "It's an answer to prayer! But how did it happen?"

"It was a miracle," replied Ma-ma simply. "There is only one point where you can see the Burma Road after the trail leaves it, and at that place the road is only a few yards in length. We were walking those few yards when Mary and Solomon were crossing over the mountain. They looked down and Mary, recognizing Danny and his carriers, called to us!"

But unknown to them, another miracle had been silently wrought on their behalf that night! The next day a runner entered the city with bad news. A Communist column had been marching down the Mekong Valley as Ma-ma and her group came down the parallel Salween Valley, and the Reds had taken and burned the bridge on the Mekong and were making for Paoshan. The city was fortified immediately. Then came word that the Salween bridge was destroyed and by Monday morning the way to the hospital had been cut off! Ma-ma's carriers had not stayed at that place all Sunday, but made an early start and were in Paoshan by the time for Sunday service. If they had not done that, and if Ma-ma had not been brought on that truck on Saturday night, they would probably have fallen into the hands of this regiment now making for Paoshan!

On Monday morning the direction the Reds were taking was not yet known, but that Mary could not now get to any hospital was obvious. The road was cut on each side, and no one knew when such big bridges could be recaptured and mended. Oldest Brother, Sister Four and Ma-ma had a consultation about Mary. Mary herself had made a decision—she wanted to go back with the carriers from Olives.

"It looks as if that is best, under the circumstances, Mary," said Ma-ma reluctantly. "But I want you to know that we have done what we could. We are wiring to Ma-pa" (who had gone out to Kunming city to see to the reprinting of the Lisu catechism and other such books and who was due to return now) "to bring with him a nasal polypus snare, and Dr. Toop says that he could operate on you in your own home at Olives, if he had that snare. They are hoping to come in and pay us a visit some time, so we will pray that it will work out that way." Mary was happy about this and the group shook hands.

"Don't you think that you should take the Middle Salween route home?" asked Ma-ma.

"Maybe," answered Junia, "but there is Solomon, who is waiting for us! Without heavy loads, we will walk fast." And with that, the little group started off.

They met many trucks of Nationalist soldiers going to the Mekong to fight, but themselves were undisturbed that first day and night. By the morning of the second day they could hear firing, and decided to make for the mountains as soon as possible. Just above the spot where Mary had seen Ma-ma's group far below on the Burma road, the firing became so loud that the little group huddled together like a flock of sheep. A noise in the bushes below them made them crouch lower. Then the bushes parted and the scared face of a Nationalist soldier appeared. He looked so frightened to see them that they grew courageous, and Junia, who could speak Chinese said, "What's going on?"

"We're fighting the Reds," answered the soldier, drawing himself up to the trail. "But I'm clearing for home. Don't you report me if you see the rest of my gang!"

"We won't. But who is winning?" asked Junia curiously.

"Don't really know, but I think we are. The battle is hottest at Wa-yao. Where are you fellows going?"

"We're from the Salween," said Junia, "and came by here to pick up one of our number who was to wait for us, but we don't see him."

"Oh he won't be here now," said the soldier. "He will have gone. The battle has been raging since last night. And you will walk right into it if you go your usual road. I know, because my home is near here. Go to that village and ask for a guide to take you up over the top of this mountain through the woods. That is your best plan." And he disappeared.

The Lisu grouped close together, asking Junia to interpret what the man had been saying, but the shooting began to get

thunderous and much closer, so Junia took command. "Everyone
to the top of this mountain; we must hide in the woods there."
And with that they ran. Mary could run too, as fleet and sure-
footed as a mountain goat, especially as she had no load to
carry; the "brethren" had seen to that. By late afternoon they
had reached the top, found a place deep in the woods where
they would be hidden from view, and attempted to build a fire
large enough to cook some rice yet small enough not to be
noticed. They could hear sounds of distant firing, so knew
that the battle was still in progress. There they spent that
November night, and long before daylight were up cooking
breakfast, so that they might be on the road by the first streaks
of day.

A native promised to guide them over the top and on to the
Tsaogien road, from where their path would be familiar. This
he did, and when they descended into that ravine where the
Tsaogien River flows, their hearts were elated, feeling that now
they were safe and the battle behind them. They had not gone
far when someone discerned another Lisu on ahead, all by himself! A second look and they recognized that it was Solomon!
Oh what a shout awakened the rocky echoes of the ravine.
Oh the joy of poor Solomon to find himself once more in the
bosom of the Olives family! That is *such* a comfortable feeling,
to be surrounded by well-known faces and voices and manners.
Then their tongues wagged as they compared notes. Solomon
waited, he told them, as under agreement, until he heard the
sound of firing, and natives running by warned him of the
approaching battle. Then, taking to his heels, he followed these
fugitives as they led him past The-Meeting-of-the-Streams
town and other usual stopping-places, which were in the line of
fire. They had pointed out the general direction of Tsaogien
and he had gradually found the road.

As they walked and talked, rounding a curve of the road
brought them without warning upon three soldiers sitting by
the roadside resting. Up went three guns. "What people?"
"Poor Lisu who carried loads," faltered Junia in his strongly
accented tribal Chinese. "We are just going home."

"Oh, then we will walk with you, for we are going toward

Tsaogien, too," said the three genially, lowering their guns and getting up for the road journey once more.

"They're brigands!" whispered Junia in Lisu to his frightened group, who huddled close to him. "I know their clothes and their caps. The bunch that robbed the lairds last May wore these.'

But the soldiers appeared very friendly, chatting and asking questions trying to find out if the Lisu had seen the fight. Junia was very guarded in his replies and purposely vague and stupid. He soon saw that they understood no Lisu, so he felt relieved that he could talk to his friends without being understood. The Communists looked hungry and worn; obviously they had had nothing to eat for some time. They explained their presence as having been lost, separated from their regiment, and hoping to find it in the hills of Tsaogien. Junia took all this in and made up his mind.

"They're weak from hunger, I bet," he said in snatches to Mary and the others. "Let's walk fast and we will outstrip them without openly running from them. Who knows where the rest of their gang is and what would happen if we met a lot of them."

Now, no man, white or Chinese, can equal the tribesman's fast dog-trot on the hills.[1] On the plain we outstrip them easily, for they say their legs hurt when they walk on the horizontal. But on the rolling hills or even the high mountains they are like the wild goats. Soon a distance began to come between the three soldiers and the small Lisu group.

"Wait for us! Don't go so fast!" called out the Reds, beginning to see what was happening. Junia muttered some excuse and the Olives band sped silently on. The Communists tried to quicken their pace, even to run, but Junia had guessed correctly, hunger had weakened them and the distance between them and the Lisu grew every moment.

"Ah you're mean! You're hearts aren't good!" they called pantingly after the fast disappearing Lisu, but it was of no avail. Chuckling, they sped out of sight. The hills gradually became lower, then fell away entirely into the mountain-girt little plain

[1] The Lisu say that Brother Three can equal them, but certainly few could.

of Tsaogien, which is the usual stopping-place. The little stream wanders slowly through the middle, and tucked in against the foot of the western hills are a few mud-housed villages. At the far end of the plain Mary could see the tower which denoted the town from which the plain gets its name.

"We had better not camp here to-night," said Junia. "He said their group were in the mountains; probably he meant the mountains to the south, but we better not take a chance. Mary, can you go still further? Can you make the Hot Springs before eating?"

"Yes," she panted shortly. "Go on. I can keep up." And so they sped on over the little plain and well into the mountains of the west toward the Salween canyon. Passing a few huts by the roadside, Junia stopped to ask, "Have you seen any soldiers lately?"

"No. Nothing since you passed by here a week ago. Everything's quiet" was the comforting reply. So by dark they had come to that little dell at the foot of the big climb, where both hot and cold water run out night and day from the bowels of the earth. No one was in sight. Dropping wearily on the ground, they stretched out for a few moments of luxurious relaxation, and then up with a spring to go and find firewood before night hid all from sight. Thirty miles they had walked that day and without daring to stop at noon for either food or rest.

"Mary, you just stay here and rest. We'll find the wood and cook the supper," said the ever-kind brethren, so she sat warming her hands gratefully as the red flames shot up, and the dry branches crackled merrily. One of the sweet joys of life is that grateful rest period when the day's labour is over and well done, and one just has to sit around the cosy warmth and chat. But to-night Mary was uneasy. At each twitter in the wooded heights above them, at each crackle of a branch under some animal foot, she started and looked uneasily at the others. They tried to appear unconcerned, but Caleb said, "Don't you think we had better try to make the river crossing at Da-han to-morrow? I'd feel safer on our own side of the Salween." There was a chorus of acquiescence, only—could Mary make it? It would be at least fifty miles, and the big climb over the pass was included. Mary was already asleep, wrapped in her blanket by the side of the fire; the comforting food, the pleasant warmth, the weariness had all combined and she was in dreamland for the night. Quietly the men chatted for a while, every now and again uneasily scanning the horizon, but as all seemed normal they were soon asleep.

Next day they did that fifty miles, Mary with them, though how she did it in her condition is nothing short of a miracle. But on the evening of that day the group rolled up in the sand on their own side of the Salween River and went to sleep comforted. The next morning Mary could not walk; her ankles were swollen and it was obvious that she could never do thirty miles that day. Nothing daunted, the brethren got some poles and made a mountain chair; some took double loads, and those thus left free carried Mary in the chair, and that night they reached—Olives! Oh the blessedness of *home. Be it ever so humble, there is no place like home.*

When Ma-ma heard this story a month later she asked anxiously. "And was Mary ill from that awful experience? It was enough to kill her—walking that distance!"

"Oh no," they replied. "After a few days' rest she was up and about her work as usual. She carried water and wove the cloth and was quite all right."

8

The Communist Stone of Fire

IT was already December before Ma-ma and Danny once again arrived home at Olives. Chungking had fallen to the Communists, and it was but a matter of time, in Ma-ma's judgment, before all China fell. It was customary for the new régime to delay missionaries at the place where the new régime found them, so if Ma-ma had been found at Paoshan, it might have been difficult to get a travel permit to return to Lisuland. Fearing this, she did not wait for Ma-pa to arrive from Kunming, but hurried home with Danny so that the new Government might find her in her rightful field. Ma-pa had already left Kunming, bringing the newly printed books with him, but how he would get across the Mekong now that the bridge was destroyed was a problem. He was bringing Eva Tseng with him. A graduate now from the Tali hospital, she had chosen to come back to do medical work among the Lisu, rather than accept any of the remunerative positions open to Chinese graduate nurses.

To her dismay, Ma-ma found Mary in bed.

"Ma-ma," Mary whispered, "I cannot retain any food. That is my worst trouble."

"Well," said Ma-ma. "Rest is the best thing. I will do all I can to help, and when Eva arrives she will doubtless be able to relieve you in other ways."

Christmas was approaching and still Ma-pa had not arrived; nor was there any word of what had happened to him and Eva. Friday the 23rd was fixed as the day of assembling, and once more the festival was to be held in Village of the Olives.

Monday of that week a small note was handed in to Ma-ma. It read:

"Dear Ma-ma,—We are coming down to 'liberate' Olives this week. Do not be afraid. I will be there in person and I have my men under control. Do not try to run and do not hide your things. You will not be harmed at all, I promise you. I hope to pass Christmas with you all. The writer is

"Red Thomas."

Shortly afterwards Gaius arrived with an imperturbable expression on his face—one he often has when good reason demands keeping counsel and being discreet. He whispered he would appreciate seeing Ma-ma privately, so as soon as possible the opportunity was given him, Lu-seng alone being allowed to remain during their talk.

"Last night when at Lameh village on a trading deal," he said, "I saw Red Thomas and Communist troops there. He says he is coming down here this week, but I noticed he is bringing many Lo-zi-lo-pa (heathen robbers) with him, so I asked the reason, and he replied that as Laird Dwan is wily he needed to be well prepared. He said that Ma-ma was not going to be annoyed and that the Lo-zi-lo-pa were under his control, but I thought you ought to know." Lameh is only a day's journey from Olives.

As this was so important a matter, neither Gaius nor Lu-seng dared to be responsible for counselling Ma-ma, but she did the best thing—asked the Lord's counsel—and after a time on her knees with the open Word of God, she felt definitely that He had given her Mal. 3:17, 18: ". . . my jewels. . . . I will spare them, as a man spareth his own son that serveth him. Then shall ye return and discern between the righteous and the wicked, between him that serveth God and him that serveth him not."

"He led me to return here," Ma-ma said simply to her anxious friends, "And I feel His word to me is that we will be kept. Except for hiding a few medicines and kerosene, I will do just as Thomas said—make no preparation but prayer."

Evening brought Brother Three, who had come to help prepare for the Christmas festival. He was disappointed that Ma-pa had not arrived, but quite agreed with Ma-ma in her stand. And so they awaited developments.

On Wednesday afternoon Lu-seng walked into Ma-ma's shanty with his face grim. "They've arrived! At least five Communists are down in Hanna's house—the vanguard, they say—and the village is to prepare food for 180 men to-night."

"What are you going to do?" asked Ma-ma.

"Don't know. The headman, Yi-hwey-pa, has escaped. Guess he is afraid because of those guns he took by force from northern Lisu this autumn! The rest of us have no guns. Here is another note for you from Red Thomas. Nathanael brought it just now. We'll be lucky if food is all we lose," he muttered half to himself, and went out by the door.

This note was like the first one; it was very affectionate and humble and assured Ma-ma she would have nothing to fear.

But at dusk Lu-seng once more appeared, his face flushed and angry. "Ma-ma, you've got to go into my house next-door. There's going to be a battle here to-night!" Then in a low whisper, and pointing down the southern trail with agitated finger, "The laird's got soldiers hidden at Shi-kwey-de." (Shi-kwey-de is a fold in the mountain on the southern trail into Olives.) "They have sent word that they are going to get those five Reds who came to order the food and that they will kill any of us who feed the Communists!"

"Well, what will you do?" whispered Ma-ma in alarm.

"The food is already cooked. We men are going to melt away out of sight. It's the only thing we can do; it is not convenient to take sides. We're carrying Mary up to Abigail's house. You and Danny go into mine!"

Lu-seng's new big two-story mud house was nearly finished. Its walls were over one foot thick, so it was bullet-proof. Ma-ma's house, having only braided bamboo mats for walls would not be safe. As a matter of fact, the big mud house, though it looked so fine, was clammy and damp inside and Mary had had to be removed to Lu-seng-ma's bamboo shanty. But under gun-fire that was not safe, so she was being carried up to the most out-of-the-way shanty. She had been unable to retain food for a month and was very weak in consequence. Ma-ma waved lovingly to her as she passed by, and a wan smile came back.

Ma-ma washed Danny in the big clay house, and as dark fell suddenly three gunshots pierced the quiet at the northern end of the dell, from which the Reds must enter. Caught in among the mountainous rocks, each shot echoed until it sounded like twenty. But after that, all was silent. The whole night passed in peace and the next morning Lu-seng appeared with a grimace.

"Somebody must have told! Not a soul of either side here this morning; all is peace. Mary wants to come back home; she feels better down here, she says."

Thursday passed in peace. Friday morning the Communists were in possession and Red Thomas with his liberation captain and a couple of soldiers stayed in Lu-seng-pa's shanty, so that Mary had to move again, this time to the old chapel next door. This, the chapel where they were married, had thick clay walls and was now being used as a church kitchen, so, being Lu-seng's property, he had placed a big granary there and made a bed on top of it for Mary. She had had some more hæmorrhages and had to lie flat all the time now. She heard Lu-seng say to Red Thomas, "Friend, I do not think you are safe here. You ought to be careful!" And Thomas had replied, "Oh I have men posted in the hills around. We're watching." But at noon gunshots in the mountain above were heard. Other shots answered them! The shooting increased, came nearer, then the voice of Yi-hwey-pa boomed down the mountain slope, "Every villager to your house! Anyone on the road at the peril of his life!" and this was followed by the "peh-peh-peh" of a machine gun! Lu-seng-ma, who was cooking in the old chapel now that her own shanty had been taken over by Communists, said to her husband, "What's that?" But before anyone could answer, the door flew open and in rushed Red Thomas. He walked up to Lu-seng-ma and signalled for her turban, "And your coat, Lu-seng-pa," he whispered, then hastily putting them on, he huddled his Communist clothing into a bag, threw it into the corner, and saying, "Look after this for me!" he disappeared out of the door. At the same time shots came fast and furious now from the upper trails going northward; Lu-seng-pa stepped to the door, took one look and said, "We're surrounded! Guess its Grandpa and Captain Tseng."

"My pig is outside. Do you think . . ." but Lu-seng-ma did not have time to finish, for the door once more was dashed open and Lu-seng appeared. Going up to Mary, he said, "Everything all right? Can I do anything for you? Well, they have ambushed the Communists and I'm sure they will beat them. I was helping Ma-ma and Danny into our house to be safe. I could see from the porch some fellows trying to climb the eastern precipice were peppered by the guns. I don't think they will make that climb! Did you see where Thomas went? He had on white trousers, and someone like that was racing across the fields trying to make the northern pass. The bullets were hitting the earth all around him, but I think he got away."

"What did he have on his head?" asked Lu-seng-ma indignantly.

"Yes; that's the only thing. He had a turban and a blue coat on, and Thomas, of course, was wearing a soldier's coat and cap."

"Oh?" drawled Lu-seng-pa, reaching for the bag thrown in the corner and pulling out Thomas' cap and coat. "He was, was he? Well, what do you suppose this is?" And then as Lu-seng excitedly recognized the clothing, the whole story was told.

"Humph," grunted Lu-seng, "We must not harbour his things here for our place will be searched. He is an old friend. I could not refuse to take him in. Well, I will bury these in the mountainside. I daren't have them around."

For four hours the fighting raged and at the end of that time the dell was quiet. Four Communists lay dead and three were captured; the rest had melted away. Then the laird's men came down off the trails and hunted through the village. It was Yi-hwey-pa all right. He had not escaped to Burma, as some thought, but had merely gone to get the laird and Captain Tseng. Other feudal lairds were joining them, but conveniently had not arrived until they saw that Dwan was going to win. Again the door of Mary's refuge was dashed open and Boanerges' heathen brother, followed by the laird's soldiers, came in and stood in front of Mary and the granary. "They're harbouring Red Thomas! I know they are. He is hiding under Mary at this very moment!" he accused excitedly. The laird's men knew

Lu-seng and hesitated, but Lu-seng himself pushed into the fast-filling room.

"My wife is sick and I won't have her scared. But neither will I put up with these lies. Give me time to get Mary down and into our shanty, and Father—you get the crowbar and open the granary! It is nailed because it is nearly filled with grain."

"Oh, don't bother," said one of the soldiers, ashamed, as Mary was wearily trying to crawl down from the high cupboard.

"No! I insist that you prove this accusation false!" demanded Lu-seng, also excited. So after the poor girl had been carried to the lower house, the granary was forced open to reveal— just unhulled rice. But it had the effect Lu-seng wished. The soldiers melted out the door shamefaced with apologies, *and no one saw the bag still huddled in the corner!*

When dark fell on that mountain dell a runner came in from the south. He brought an important piece of news, a Government document, notifying the feudal lairds that the Governor of Yunnan Province had submitted to the Communists and that now *the whole province was under the new régime, and calling upon them to submit also!*

If only that runner had come at noon! The blood of the Communists was not yet dry on the ground, and here was news that all China had now fallen to them. Feudal lairds in a remote little valley—how could they possible hope to hold it against the whole of China?

The lairds had made their beds in Lu-seng's house, of course. They always took over the best place in the village. Brother Three, who had not yet his own cabin, at Lu-seng's invitation, was occupying the upper room under which the lairds were to sleep. Until midnight he heard them discussing their problem: how would they gain face with the new régime after the battle of that afternoon? Before dawn they had their solution —they picked on the weak place in Red Thomas' plans, the *Lo-zi-lo-pa* he had brought with him. "They weren't Communists we fought," they decided to publish. "*They were well known robbers. We were protecting the people.*" And so when Saturday morning arrived and Ma-ma arose to meet the new

day, Brother Three told her at the breakfast table the astounding
news that "Grandpa" now was also a Red!

"I can't keep my face straight when I think of it," he said.
"They calmly announced to me just now that they are Communists too—since last night!"

"Well, what has been worrying me," said Ma-ma anxiously,
"are those three boys they have captured, and some say they
are going to kill them. Why, they are new believers who were
coming to spend Christmas with us. Yesterday was assembling
day, you remember. Do you think those boys were Communists?"

"They met Thomas and accepted his badge. That is what
makes it impossible for me to do anything."

"Yes, but they did not know all that the badge implied,"
Ma-ma argued anxiously. "Thomas is a Christian. He said he
was coming to celebrate Christmas here too. They don't understand this political fight."

"Well, we certainly must try and do something," said Brother
Three. "Especially for little Bo-to; he is only fifteen years old."
Whereupon the two missionaries prayed and light was given
them in this darkness.

Brother Three went to Laird Dwan and Ma-ma to another
laird, but the gist of their plea was the same. They said quietly
that the group ambushed yesterday were most certainly Communists, for they had talked personally with Red Thomas, and
since the lairds themselves were now submitting to the new
régime it would be the part of wisdom to deal leniently with
those captured. This took the lairds' excuse away, and again
they consulted together, coming to the decision to ask for a
peace-party and that Brother Three accept the position of
guarantor that this was not a trick, but *bona-fide*. He did so
gladly, so each of them drew up a paper to this effect and
stamped it with their personal seals. Then came the question
the missionaries had been hoping for: who is going to take
the letter asking for a truce?

Not a soul of the laird's party was willing to go north into
the mountains and hunt for the chagrined and angry Communists!

"Why not let young Bo-to take it?" the missionaries suggested. This was hailed with pleasure as a fine solution, and so Bo-to was freed and started on his journey. After a few hours of bustle, the lairds withdrew and the Village of Olives was at last in peace. It was Christmas Day.

But peace was short-lived. The next day a letter, addressed to Ma-ma, but really meant for the village, arrived, signed by Red Thomas. It was a very angry letter, accusing Olives of treachery and saying there was no use to refute the charge as he, Red Thomas, knew all about it and the names of those who had played false, and revenge was sure. With that letter came an oral word that the *Lo-zi-lo-pa* were to be let loose upon Olives to kill, plunder, loot—anything they liked that could be reckoned as punishment! This time it really appeared that Olives was in danger. The lairds and their men had withdrawn; the *Lo-zi-lo-pa* were noted for their ferocity and ruthlessness, the most dreaded robbers in the canyon, and there was good looting, for Olives had just harvested splendid crops of rice and cotton. This time a temporary withdrawal seemed the wisest course; but that morning Ma-ma had been struck by a verse on her calendar. It was *"Leave not thy place,"* Eccles. 10:4. It had come with that impress of the spirit which accompanies the voice of the Lord.

"I do not know why, but I believe God has told me not to run," she said.

"Well, I can't run," said Lu-seng. "Mary is in no condition for such. We must stay, whatever happens. After the fighting on Friday she had two hæmorrhages and was unconscious."

Brother Three said that he certainly was not going to run, and so they waited, hour after hour, even for several days, trusting the Lord to undertake, which He did.

The man in white trousers who successfully dodged those many bullets was not Thomas after all, but a local cowherd on his way home! Thomas had hidden himself in Lu-seng's haystack by the road to the waterhole. All night he lay concealed there, and as everyone went up that trail to get water for supper, and were discussing the affair, Thomas learned everything. He learned how Yi-hwey-pa had run to summon Laird Dwan, which of the heathen villagers had helped, pointing out where the Reds were hiding—he had learned everything, just as he said. But before the *Lo-zi-lo-pa* were let loose, little Bo-to with his peace letters had arrived and that changed the complexion of the whole situation. No telegraph or telephone, not even a daily postal system—there was no way by which Thomas could inform Ma-ma that the proposals were accepted until she received word that the Communist truce party were already in the village and on their way up to her shanty for an interview with her! In that one hour she received a second piece of news— namely, *that the lairds had changed their mind.* They had heard that truce would mean that they must hand over their guns, and that, Laird Dwan said, he would never do! The messenger casually added that one of the peace party already ascending the hill to see Ma-ma was a *Communist woman soldier!* That, to Ma-ma, was like the last straw. She pictured a young Amazon-with-a-pitchfork type of female, and her heart sank, but they were almost there.

Dusk had fallen as the Communist party entered. Ma-ma's first anxious glance searched for the woman soldier; then she gave a sigh of relief, for she was just a slightly built Chinese student girl in the usual blue cotton gown, big rain-hat, and cloth slippers on her feet. The villagers, heathen as well as Christian, were pouring into the shanty, so Ma-ma slipped toward a seat at the side.

"Fasten that door open!" commanded the Koh-chang— deputy officer of a department. The door was obediently tied back by one of his men. The party consisted of four, the Koh-chang, the young captain who had been ambushed, Red Thomas, and the girl soldier. Ma-ma offered tea. The three men took it brusquely, but the girl refused it. Coming in last, she had taken a seat at the table next the door, the seat usually occupied by Ma-ma at breakfast, and Ma-ma made a mental note, "She'll catch cold, for when that door is open that seat is right in a big draught." But more important matters were at stake: would the Laird Dwan ambush again? But the Koh-chang was speaking.

"Madam, which of my men robbed you?"

"None, sir," was Ma-ma's quiet reply.

"Then why did you kill them?"

"We did not, sir, and the lairds say they mistook you for robbers." Ma-ma decided she would say no more; the Lisu heathen who were responsible were sitting beside her.

"Those lairds have too much power," snarled the Koh-chang. "The way they oppress these poor people! Boycotting them on salt, making women carry injurious loads up steep mountains so that they can fatten themselves by a better salt market. . . ." and he went on. Ma-ma sat upright and listened. Where had he learned all that? This was interesting, and so far it was true. But as he went on, relating various incidents that had taken place within the last six months, an old sinner at Ma-ma's left began to get uncomfortable, for the Koh-chang was hitting him too, and at last he put in a word. It was an excuse, soft and flatteringly couched in nice words, but almost slimy with falseness. The girl soldier had been silent up to this point, but as that suave, slippery effort to escape judgment ended, she straightened, turned and flashed a fire that made the old sinner cower back. She did not yell, her voice was low and cultured, but she just whipped off the veil with which he had tried to hide his deeds, exposed it for what it was, and with short, scathing contempt turned back to her previous haughty silence.

"My goodness, you can talk when you want to," thought Ma-ma to herself. "That was magnificently done, and like a lady too. I wonder who you are, and how you came into this wild canyon with such company?" Then, as she watched, suddenly a vision of Joan of Arc flashed into her mind. "Why, bless your heart, you're a little old patriot. That explains it. I hope you don't catch cold in that draught! I'd like to get you a coat. No, I'd better not; they will think I'm toadying. I don't want to be classed with this hypocrite here. I'd better keep my hands off." And so Ma-ma settled back to listen to the Koh-chang, who was now discussing politics with a stranger who sat on Ma-ma's right. By and by the Communist girl began to sniffle.

"Yes, you are catching cold all right," Ma-ma's mental soliloquy went on. "It's too bad that such an earnest little thing should get sick. She may be deluded, but she's made of good stuff. Wonder if I dare chance it? Yes, I will." And without warning Ma-ma ran up the ladder to the loft where she slept, and returned with a coat.

"I am afraid you are catching cold," she said pleasantly and proffered the garment.

In a second that girl had stiffened and thrown up her hands in a gesture of icy refusal.

The Koh-chang was a bit ashamed. "Oh, she is all right, madam. She is tough. She travels the road with us men, sleeps by the roadside if we have to. We came from Ma-pu-la-de to-day. She can take it."

"That is not it, sir," replied Ma-ma putting the proffered coat aside. "That is my seat at mealtimes, and when the door is open there is a big draught there. She has been mountain climbing and is heated; I was afraid that she would catch cold. That is all. *You* are not in danger, for the draught only hits her seat."

Then Ma-ma sat down, but as she did so she noticed that the student girl had at last taken in Ma-ma's real motive. She flushed a rosy red to the roots of her hair, turned as if to apologize, though still not accepting the coat. "Hm," thought Ma-ma. "She did not understand. She thought it was American patronage of her apparent poverty. Well, I like her. Wish I could get a chance to talk to her."

In the meantime the crowd had been gradually leaving. Red Thomas was warned that the lairds were reported to have changed their minds, and he hastily called his comrades into the room assigned for their sleeping quarters. Unknown to Ma-ma, Lu-seng had also called a secret meeting of the deacons. "We are not Communists," he informed them, "but in the person of our white missionaries we have pledged our honour that this peace party shall not meet with treachery. I can see no other way than that we men guard all the trails leading in to this village all night, so that they will not be surprised by an attack. I want five men for each trail, and I myself will join one group. Once daylight comes, the peace party must take its chances; we will have fulfilled our part."

This was done. On his way by the window of the house

where the Communists were sitting around their fire, Lu-seng overheard one of them say fearfully to the others, "Are you sure that Laird Dwan is not even right now hiding in some friendly hut in the village?" but Red Thomas assured them not. He had learned of the action of the church—a December night in the mountains to stand guard all night was no small thing.

The next morning dawned clear and sunny, and all had been peaceful. Ma-ma overhead the young Communist captain say to someone, "Well, they are not all bad men in this village! If you ask me, most of them are a rare good sort!" She smiled to herself: "They must have learned about the guards last night."

By ten o'clock the road ahead had been examined and pro-nounced clear, and Red Thomas called the peace party to gather for departure. Ma-ma went out and, seeing the girl soldier standing by herself looking over the little dell, she went up to her.

"How old are you, Yang Lao-si?"

"Twenty-one," was the smiling reply.

"I have a daughter in America who is a student too, and you make me think of her."

"Lady Teacher, we Communists and you are brothers. I think you have done a wonderful work in reducing this Lisu language to writing, and also the whole effect of your work has been most impressive to me. I came down over the ninth district" (which is almost all heathen) "and then into your Christian district, and I could not but see the difference between the heathen Lisu and the Christian Lisu. The heathen are opium sots, liars, thieves, you cannot depend on them. The Christians are so different; they are like us. So I say, we are brothers."

"Well, my dear," answered Ma-ma slowly, "there are simi-larities without any doubt. But as I see it, it is like this. You Communists are trying to change men's conduct. You want equality, all having the same chances in life. Christ wants that too, but He *changes men's hearts*. If you only force a change in conduct, you have not solved your problem. It will break out again. But if you change men's hearts the conduct rights itself just naturally. All our Christians were heathen to start with."

Miss Yang looked thoughtful. Then her face cleared. "Oh,

yes, but we are going to change men's hearts too," she exclaimed. "We are going to change men's hearts too!" Just at that moment her comrades called her to join them, so Ma-ma gave her a couple of tracts, which she started to read tripping happily down the trail.

Ma-ma stood and watched her go with a yearning in her heart. "You are a dear and I pity you," she soliloquized. "You are obviously an idealist; that explains it. I suppose it is only the idealist who would offer to liberate such a place as this canyon is. But you are bound to disappointment if you think that man can change man's heart. You can change man's *thinking* with your careful indoctrinations, but that has not changed his heart, little girl! 'For men shall be lovers of their own selves . . . without natural affection . . . truce-breakers . . . having a form of godliness, but denying the power thereof.' Wait until your life's happiness is in the hands of such, and you will find your hopes turned to ashes. You will find that, though the thinking has changed, the sin is still there, the corruption is still going on, the man is still undependable. It was not a mere change in thinking that made opium-smokers, thieves and liars into the Christians who guarded you last night! You poor child. Disillusionment is a bitter experience. You will have no hope left unless . . . unless you remember that in Lisuland you *did* see hearts and conduct permanently changed by One called Christ. And you saw honour and love *at work*, not just talking. You do not know that it is Christ who only can make men brothers; it is Christ alone who really cares for the under-dog. You heard of His principles under the borrowed name of Communism, and, falling in love with Him, that is what brought you into this canyon, just as that is what brought me. I would like to be on the Lisu trail when you come back disillusioned. I would like to help you find Him.

"But you have been a real challenge to me too. You have deliberately stripped yourself of privileges you might have had in order to come down to the level of the Lisu people. You walk their trails (thirty miles you did yesterday; that is superb) and sleep on their board beds, eating their coarse food without a murmur, never asking for anything better. I've been disgruntled sometimes lately because living conditions continue so rough: that old ladder, the smoke, the draughts and so on. But I see now it was the Lord's kindness to me, so that I might not have to blush in your presence. You are tough, the Koh-chang said. Disciplined, he meant. I would that the Western world accept the challenge of your life, or they will never be your victor in the end."

It will take *stones of fire* to conquer Communism.

One brave missionary who elected to stay behind with the Chinese Church when others of her mission were withdrawing wrote: "We must out-love, out-serve, out-sacrifice any others who claim to have a way to solve life's problems."

9

From His Pocket to His Crown

MA-MA was distinctly worried about Mary's condition. For over a month now she had not been able to retain food, and the polypus was growing like nothing Ma-ma had ever seen. It was also septic. If only Ma-pa and Eva would come!

Then one day (January 8th, 1950) they were sighted coming along the winding trail into Olives! What a reunion that was; but before nightfall Ma-ma led Eva into Lu-seng-ma's hut, where Mary now lay.

"Do you remember Sister Eva who taught you how to knit in Girls' Bible School in 1943?" Ma-ma said gently.

Mary smiled her wan smile and reached out a pitifully thin hand. Hope was high in every breast as Eva turned her flashlight on that throat.

"No; I have never seen anything like this before" she said. "All my three years in the Tali Hospital we never had a case like this. But I will use what medicines I have and we will see." Then everything that love and medical skill could devise was done to make Mary comfortable, and she felt so much better that in a few days' time she even sat up outside in the sunshine.

But one night, as it was nearing dawn, Lu-seng-pa called Ma-ma and Eva. Mary's little daughter was still-born. Again Nurse Eva's skill helped the weak and fainting mother, and now that the cause of the nausea was gone, hope once more soared. But the polypus had gone down into the throat and speech was blocked. Mary signalled to Eva and asked her to try to operate, for there was Samuel Ju, also a graduate, who could be called in to assist. If only that polypus were out, Mary felt that she would begin to get strong again. Ma-pa had responded to the telegram and the necessary instrument was now right in the village.

To comfort her, Ma-ma agreed, and two Lisu were sent the six days' journey to Paoshan city to bring back an anæsthetic and medical instructions. There was no hope that the doctor could come when the countryside was so upset politically. Indeed Ma-ma knew that this was merely a gesture of sympathy to comfort the sick one; even two graduate nurses could hardly perform such an operation.

Mary's patience and fortitude were wonderful. Always her New Testament and the hymn-book she had won as Bible Club award lay on a ledge near her hand, and with all her physical misery there was still an atmosphere of rest and quietness. The only time Ma-ma knew her to be angry or display emotion was when Martha or heathen relatives began to wail like heathen do. Then her eyes flashed fire and an imperious wave of the hand was more eloquent than speech. She forbad them.

Once when feeling very weak she signed to Ma-ma, and as Ma-ma bent over her, Mary waved her hand from herself up to the sky, then put her hands together in the attitude of prayer, closed her eyes a moment, then opened them and looked keenly to see if her message had been understood.

Ma-ma nodded and right there, prayed that if it were not God's will to make her better, He would take her quickly to Himself. When the prayer was over, Mary smiled and formed her lips into the Lisu words for "Thank you," and the peace once more reigned on her face.

The messengers from Paoshan were already on the return journey when one night, January 28th, 1950, about 2.0 o'clock, Timothy came underneath Ma-ma's window and called her.

"Mary has fallen asleep," he said.

"Praise God," replied Ma-ma, even though there was that human stab of the heart when a loved one leaves us. "Did she suffer?"

"No," he replied. "We were all asleep, when Lu-seng-pa woke up and realized that the rattle-breathing from Mary's bed, which has been constant night and day for a couple of weeks now, had stopped. The room was silent. He got some pine chips, lit them and found—she was gone. Are you coming down to sing the death song?"

When the Lisu Christians depart, instead of the heathen's death wail, their brethren in Christ gather around and sing, "Sleep on, beloved." It was a quavering little chorus that dawn, for this one and then that one would break down for a second, then try to take it up again. It is not easy to say goodbye.

Just twenty-five years old! Oh why did God let it happen? He has not yet explained the reason. But if the great Gem-Lover decided that He wanted to transfer this little stone of fire from His pocket to His crown, who dare say Him nay? In His pocket it is sweet to His touch, but in His crown myriads can enjoy it, who would otherwise not even know it existed. And what a joy for her! To go to sleep in that little dark hut; then, a touch on her shoulder. She looks up and sees the King in His beauty, His radiance, filling the poor little cluttered hut, until, like soft moonlight, it had blurred out the ugliness and merged all objects into a soothing dimness.

"Come," said that Loved One. "Enter into the joy of your Lord."

And the shining hosts behind Him, smiling and longing to come closer to escort her? Boanerges' adult daughter and son. Azor's first wife. Yes, she was not leaving the dear brethren of Olives; she was just joining the other part of their family.

Did she turn and give one quick glance at that emaciated form on the bed? Her old earthly clothes, that body was. Oh what joy to be free from it, to take a deep breath of the exhilarating nectar of heaven. "Yes, O wondrous Captain of my salvation, and dear heavenly friends, I am ready. Let us be gone!"

> *"Then forth on joyful wing cleaving the sky,*
> *Sun, moon, and stars forgot, upward I fly."*

From His pocket to His crown. Dare anyone say it was not fair?

The strains of the Christian death song floating through the cold dawn of that mountain village announced to all what had happened. In no time Martha was flying over the trail, weeping as she came. Once at the bedside, she lapsed into the old heathen death chanting, quite unconscious that it was exactly what Mary would not have wanted. "My little sister, I will not see you again," she wailed rocking back and forth till Ma-ma went and shook her, trying to bring her to her Christian senses, but a dazed upward look was all the reply. Martha's soul was in the days gone by, wandering through the memory lanes of childhood, calling, calling for the one who had always been at her side.

Never in all her sixteen years in the canyon had Ma-ma heard such a mourning as took place. For three days, late into the night and before daylight, someone was wailing. Even Lu-seng could not stop it, and as no grave was ready he could not shorten the mourning until all was prepared. The heathen of course, made the greatest noise, for the real Christian does not wail.

Several times Ma-ma went down to the hut to see if she could help. One such time the room was empty, but Lydia had entered just ahead of Ma-ma, so preoccupied that she never saw who was following her. Ma-ma stopped at the door and watched.

Lydia went softly up to the coffin and drew back the sheet from the placid young face. She gazed and gazed and then hot tears began to drop. Long did she stand there, unconscious of an audience, weeping silently over Mary's face. Ma-ma tiptoed away with a prayer of gratitude in her heart. " 'To meddle is to muddle'—the Great Lover of souls has His own ways of awakening us," she thought.

When at last all was ready and the pall-bearers were called in line (stalwart youths of Olives, heathen as well as Christian had offered) one of the tallest and biggest of them was crying out aloud like a five-year-old. Lu-seng, eyes red and swollen, had previously brought in to Ma-pa a wooden cross, which he had made himself. "Please print on this—'She finished her course triumphantly,' " he said, then quickly turned and ran away.

At the close of the little service at the open grave, Lu-seng, who had been weeping, pulled himself together, and stepped forward. "I wish to say a word," he said. "I want to explain the words on the cross. Some of you are heathen and know not the power of the Lord. But you all know that Mary never faltered in her faith. You know how she suffered. You know that she never complained. It is only God that can strengthen us to finish like that." Then there followed a simple exhortation of the heathen present—and within a week two of them had turned to the Saviour. Fire from God's opal was still kindling hearts.

* * *

Just one more scene. It was at the foot of the great eleven-thousand-foot pass over which Ma-ma and Danny had to go in order to reach America. Rain had fallen and that brought an early darkness, so that there was nothing to do but go to bed. The party had arrived at the last human habitation before crossing the great peaks, and as the carriers and all were thirteen in number, quarters were cramped. Ma-ma had put Danny to bed, and had also retired with him. Next their bed was an open fire, still glowing from the fuel which cooked the evening meal. On the other side of the fire was another plank bed, occupied by Lu-seng and Caleb. Darkness, soot, cupboards and junk filled every space, and outside the drip, drip of rain on soft mud made adventure impossible, so both young men were stretched out on their bed too. Not sleepy, not able to move around, Caleb, usually a silent boy in Olives, began to talk;

"Mary, that wife of yours, was wonderful." Ma-ma lying in the dark on the other side of the fire, threw the blanket back so she could listen better. But Caleb did not notice; he was lost in memory and the privacy of the darkness made it easy for him, for once, to talk his thoughts out loud. "I cannot tell you how I miss her. I did not feel it as much when my own mother died. Somehow you expect the old folks to drop off, some time. You know it is coming. But the companion of your childhood! When I herd the cows up there on that knoll and come upon her grave, it is like a knife in my heart. She was always such a help to me. She was so faithful, always in her place in church, rain or shine, and even there she helped me. A look from Mary steadied a fellow. She did not know it, but many times, when the talk might be getting boisterous or something, just the expression on her face would straighten me up. And she always cared so much if anything happened to any of us. Our sorrow was her sorrow. And she was so pure—she never knew how much she helped me to go straight! I miss her even yet. I can't seem to get over it." And so on for about half an hour. He talked so fast, and brought up village incidents with which Ma-ma was not acquainted, so that now and again she lost the trend of it, but invariably he came back to the same point. When Mary died, something which had strengthened and blessed him was found to be gone. The darkness hid Lu-seng's face, but once, when a pause seemed to expect a remark from him, he said in a low voice, "She had wonderful endurance."

That little stone of fire was like a meteor. As it shot up to God it left a trail of light behind it which surprised everybody. The village had not realized what a spiritual prop the quiet maiden was until there came the desire to lean again, and the prop was missing.

God needs more stones of fire to-day. He can quarry them anywhere, and He does not need rare materials with which to make them; desert dust, sand, silica, these can be found anywhere: "Principle shot through with passion; passion held by principle." There must be a yielding before it will hold. There must be an offering before the fire falls. The rest is the work of the Master lapidary.

The stone is only a stone until its heart is broken and the air has a chance to get in. The Christian convert is only a principle until he lets God have His way with him; break his heart, if that has to be! Anything, in order to rip open the hardness and let God in! When the air has filled the fissures, then the stone is no longer a pebble. It is a gem, a precious opal, a stone of fire.